LaQuanda E. Brabson

BROKEN GRACEFULLY

How To Pick Up The Pieces And Still Stand Again

By

LaQuanda E. Brabson

Although the author has made every effort to ensure that the information in this book was correct at the time of first publication, the author does not assume and hereby disclaims any liability to any party for any loss, damage, or disruption caused by errors or omissions, whether such errors or omissions result from negligence, accident, or any other cause.

Copyright 2019 by LaQuanda Brabson

All rights reserved. No part of this book may be reproduced or transmitted in any form or by any means, electronic or mechanical, including photocopying, recording, or any information storage and retrieval system, without permission in writing from the author.

Printed in the United States of America

All scriptures quoted are from the Holy Bible-Youversion (Public Domain). Used by permission

Copyright 2006-2015 The Android open Source Project

Copyright 2012, 2014 google, Inc.

Graphic Design by Bishop Re'Mix|

bishopremix@gmail.com, Facebook.com/thebishopremix|

tg23designs@gmail.com

Additional graphic design by Dr. Leandre Coles of D&K Productions| DrDray Intelligent Tycoon Coles on Facebook| dkp.intelligentproduction@yahoo.com

Editorial services by Jessica Reese, MBA| @Jessica Reese for Facebook, @ mamateach for IG, and https://www.linkedin.com/in/jessica-reese-7a741320 for LinkedIn

This book is dedicated to every woman who has endured, who has lost the fight, or who is still enduring any abuse that has left her broken. By the end of this book, hopefully you are inspired to put the pieces back together again, and with God, to keep standing!

    R.I.P to the women who didn't survive!

Table of Contents

Introduction—————————————————————6

PART I: In the Beginning

Chapter One: The Relationship——————————————10

Chapter Two: Dwelling Place———————————————30

Chapter Three: Wrong Turn————————————————47

Chapter Four: The Plea——————————————————64

PART II: For the Necessary is Now

Chapter Five: The Turnaround———————————————79

Chapter Six: Unexplainable moves of Faith——————————93

PART III: The Permissive Will

Chapter Seven: Follow the Instructions————————————172

Chapter Eight: Mending the Broken Pieces——————————209

Chapter Nine: The Birthing Season—————————————230

Epilogue/Conclusion———————————————————255

Acknowledgement—————————————————————264

Additional Reading————————————————————268

About the Author—————————————————————279

Introduction

This book will take you on a journey through the life of a woman who has been broken *gracefully*. You will see how she went from a love gone wrong to her Cinderella love story. You will see how she learned what healthy love is after suffering abuse, low self-esteem, and shame.

Oblivious to the journey that God had in store for her, she didn't know how to fight in the spirit, so instead she fought in the flesh. Eventually, she decided to totally surrender to Christ and accept that the tests and trials she faced were all a part of the process. That woman became a survivor. That woman is me.

The Lord had given me this book to write in 2008, and every time I thought it was the last chapter, a new chapter would surface; so, I put the book on pause. I originally wanted to name it, *To Be in My Husband's Arms*, but He had something else in mind. On Oct 18, 2017, around 6:00am, the Lord woke me up; and in my time of prayer, He gave me a new name for the book along with a scripture. I Googled the name to see if anyone had it, and thankfully, it was not taken. What I did find though, was a song that I had heard, but I didn't know it was called *Gracefully Broken*. Since I was the one who had been adding to the chapters, I knew that I had to be the one to bring the book to a close. I was also fueled by the fact that I wasn't the only woman who had gone through this. This gave me more of an impetus to bring this book to a close. I had to share with other women how I survived the obstacles caused by domestic abuse, and I also wanted to use my testimony as a way to prevent domestic abuse. I pray you will learn how to survive your test with the word of God given throughout this book. I pray you will receive something out of each chapter. What is written are the parts that the Lord has given me permission to share.

There is a lot more that hasn't been released. As you journey through this book, you may laugh, you may cry, you may get angry, and you may be in disbelief; but know one thing: each and every chapter was necessary for the now!

Because the events in this book are inspired by prayer and the Word of God, I have included footnotes with the Biblical verses that are relevant to that time period.

> (The beginning of this book was based on a lot of past events; therefore, there will be vulgar language used from that time.)

PART I: In the Beginning

It wasn't until I took that first step that God began to work on my behalf. The love was gone, the care I had for him was gone, and the reality of my having to take a stand wasn't until I begin to make a move. It was like David when he changed his clothes. *2nd Samuel 12:20: "Then David arose from the earth, washed, anointed himself, and came into the house of the Lord, and worshipped: then he came to his own house; and when he required, they set bread before him, and he did eat" (KJV)*

Chapter One: The Relationship

Lindsey Brown trembled as her cool hands grasped the cold trigger of the 12-gauge shotgun. Not because she was afraid; she was confident, hellbent on ending the life of the man who was responsible for all the wrong turns her life had taken. She had been beaten, hospitalized, humiliated, and drugged. So, this tremble wasn't one of fear. It was one of rage. Her eyes were lowered and sinister, and her lips were squeezed in by her clenched jaws. *How did a gentile and ambitious young girl come to this?* She had gone out that day for a bag of chips, and when she came back to her home, the home she had shared with her husband and the father of her children; she was met with the stench of some other woman, *again.*

Broken Gracefully

It was the summer of 1988 in the Motor City. Sweaty enough to go shirtless or chase the ice cream truck but dry enough to avoid being inside until the street lights came on. A Detroit summer only meant a couple of things: hoodlums were committing crimes, families were piled up in American-made cars on their way to Belle Isle, kids were getting wet by the fire hose, and of course, people were falling in love. Lindsey Brown and Wesley Brooks were two such people. They were teenagers in love. They had just graduated from Lessenger Middle School, and like any young couple in this predicament, they made grown-up plans. They had made plans to attend college in North Carolina, they had made plans to get married, and they had made plans to have kids; but that was not the plan that God had in store for them because just as quickly as it began, that 2-year love ended.

It was mid-summer and Lindsey and her girls were walking in Jaybone Wise's neighborhood, Plymouth and Shaefer. On the outside, it may have appeared to be Any Urban Neighborhood, America; but for Detroiters, the quaint two-story homes, convenience stores and chicken shacks, the bumpy sidewalks and proud faces made this neighborhood infamous; just walking up and down the street would make one feel as if their summer days were well-spent. Jaybone and Wesley were neighbors who had known each other well before puberty set in. But even though they were from the same "hood", they were cut from a very different cloth - completely opposite in personality. Jaybone was the mayor of this intersection, equally adored by both men and women. He was of medium height and dark-skinned and a bit rough around the edges. But he had this baby face, and he always wore a heart-melting smile through large, nearly crooked, blindingly white teeth. He wore crisp denim jeans, a white tee shirt, and pearly white Adidas Top Tens, the typical uniform of a grown-up kid in Detroit; but he wasn't Lindsey's type. Wesley had been a tall, light-skinned golden-haired honor student. Dark-skinned bad boys simply didn't make the cut. Still, he had something. He had such an aura surrounding him that one almost forgot that he was a bit...goofy. Still, he had a head nod for everyone, and a secret handshake for those closest to him. In other words, lanky or not, he had *swag*.

It was one for one and everybody was "straight". Two of the boys, one being Jaybone, had made a bet about who would get Lindsey once Wesley and she broke up. Of course she didn't like either of them. Their rough-edged image did not mix well with Lindsey's pristine one. She was the all-around honor roll student, the church-going girl, and her mother's only child. She was well-loved, beautiful, and a leader amongst her peers. But not many young teens could pass up the magnetic pull of walking a Detroit neighborhood: fresh kicks, fly hair, a new outfit, and the stress of tests, papers, and piles of homework behind them. Not to mention the gratitude of warm weather, a rarity in Detroit. So even if she had walked the neighborhood with boys of whom her mother would never approve, she was free, she was young, and she was happy. Perhaps it was the appeal of their dissimilar personas, or it could have been proximity - they worked together at KFC - but eventually, one of the boys won her over.

"You waiting for your ride?" Jaybone asked with a menacing smirk.

"Yeah."

"I'll take you home," he said. *The rat trap.*

That one ride went from once, to once every three days. One of those rides turned into a kiss; that kiss turned into a movie date; and as it often follows, that movie date turned into, "how long you gonna' make me wait?" After 90 days, her and Jaybone made love; and there had been no turning back.

"You hear me?" Jaybone nudged Lindsey, who had been busy studying for her Chemistry test. "I don't want you to have to worry about anything. I'm going to take care of you, of us."

Lindsey beamed at this prospect. She was a serious student – anticipating graduation and intently focused on maintaining her "A" average. Jaybone continued on, dreaming up plans to buy her dream car and living a life of luxury. He had the potential too. He was charismatic and capable and hard-working.

It was another one of those Detroit summers, and Jaybone and Lindsey were approaching a red light in his blue 1983 Ford Fairmont while driving down Grand River, a street as robust and action packed as its name – salons, boutiques, repair shops, food stops, *life*. They were enjoying the Motor City in their own innocent way when suddenly a car pulled up next to them with its music blasting. Lindsey turned her head to look at the car when a hand forcefully slid across her face.

"Ain't no woman of mines gonna be looking at another nigga." Jaybone's cool voice turned dark and chilly. Lindsey made futile attempts to catch her breath, but struggled to wrap her head around what had transpired. Days ago, they were parked on tiny gravel next to minivans and pickup trucks at the drive-in on Ford ave., thinking up plans and dreams.

"Take me home now!" Lindsey exclaimed with tears running down her face, "I mean now!" As he drove back home, his tone shifted, rage turned into gentility, and Lindsey's ears were serenaded with the sincerest of apologies.

"I'm sorry, I'm sorry, don't go," he begged. She didn't budge.

When Jaybone and she finally arrived at their destination, she got out of the car without a word. She had made a vow to herself to never tolerate abuse - she had already witnessed so much with the women in her family. Still, Jaybone persisted. He would call. She ignored it. At work he would abandon his station just to get close to her, just to have a word. She walked in the other direction. He didn't give up though, steadily apologizing and promising to never do it again. After what seemed like the 100th apology and 1,000th plea, she gave in. A combination of his smile, his sincerity, and his swag had won her over.

They continued to date as if nothing had happened, and he assured her that it never would again. He would shower her with gifts and take her to beautiful places, and she happily obliged, enjoying the attention. As time passed, their bellies full of butterflies, their minds toward the future, he eventually introduced her to his family. They were a kind, hospitable, and educated middle class bunch. His sisters were beautiful as was his mom, Linda, who wore a pleasant smile. His parents were divorced, but his dad still came around.

"I like her. She's pretty." His dad told Jaybone, which left Lindsey speechless. He went on to say, "D#%* girl! What size bra you wear!" To that Jaybone and his father erupted in laughter while Lindsey's face turned beet red. She quickly learned where Jaybone inherited his sometimes crass, sometimes hilarious sense of humor. She also noticed something else. Jaybone had disrespected both his mother and his sisters. It seemed like out of nowhere that he shouted a string of F-bombs and proclamations that they never cared about him.

"Oh, you're a good one, cause ain't no way I would be with him!" one of his sisters said. When they got back in the car, she told him, "if you talk to them like that, I know you're gonna talk to me like that."

"No," he cried. "You don't understand. My momma treats me differently cause I look like my daddy and my sister always on her side. Only my older sister is in my corner. They treat me like the black sheep of the family." That's when she felt sorry for him and believed that she could help him.

That was Jaybone. Both charming and aggressive. Both tender and rough. When he laid his eyes upon a woman, she was trapped in his gaze – she could see all of the roses but also the thorns; and instead of that being frightening, it made him even more alluring; he became someone she could protect and adore. All of those things made her ignore the red flags telling her to get out.

College letters had been flooding her mailbox, which was a welcomed distraction from her relationship with Jaybone. She figured her hopes and dreams and plans for her future could balance the volatility of their relationship. Their relationship went on as it always had, but more and more she found herself inexplicably exhausted. She decided to take a pregnancy test just to rule it out. It was positive. Lindsey Brown was 17 and pregnant. She had already been four months when she found out. Even though she loved Jaybone and was unresistant to his charms, this was not supposed to happen to her. Her story was not supposed to include being a teenage mother. She refused to tell her family for fear of disappointing them, so she went to see a judge to grant her permission to have an abortion as she was just shy of 18, the legal age to have one without parental consent. The ride to the courthouse was monotonous. People walking here, kids playing there, the bus crowded with school kids and work goers. She sat staring out the foggy window wondering how she'd gotten in this situation, touching her belly as if it were a foreign object. As the bus glided down Puritan Ave., she saw billboards that read "Life, What a Beautiful Gift" and "No Abortion. Do not Kill" as well as others along those same guilt-laden lines. Before, she had taken this route without concern. But not this time. This time those signs gleamed right into her soul. When she got to the courthouse, she explained to the judge that she had plans to attend college and that having a child would be antithetical to that, so he granted her plea to have the procedure done.

On a Friday, Lindsey and Jaybone went to the abortion center. Heavy heads filled the waiting room, which was a sea of sorrow and angst. She picked up the clipboard and began filling out the mandatory questionnaire, a conscientious technicality before making an impossible decision. It read:

> Do you believe in abortions? No
>
> Do you feel abortions are right in your situation? No
>
> Do you feel your mind and heart agree with this abortion? No

No. No. No. Lindsey's mind felt that she was making the right decision. The logical decision. Her heart and soul was telling her otherwise. She had grown up in a religious

Christian family who did not believe in abortions. After the receptionist read her list of "no's", she calmly told her that they would not be able to complete the procedure but explained that once her mind and heart were in agreement that she could come back to have it done.

Lindsey left and headed out to the lobby where Jaybone was awaiting her.

"You done already?" he said.

"Yep, let's go," she replied. "I didn't have it done. Take me to my pastor's house." So, he took her.

They arrived at her pastor's house and before she could get a word out, she asked, "You pregnant?" Lindsey told her that she was and they began to talk. She explained to Lindsey how this was not the end for her and how the baby was not a sin but that the act of conception was. She didn't ridicule her. She didn't chastise her. She simply sat and listened. She also asked Lindsey if she wanted to break the news to her mom, which was something that Lindsey had been dreading.

Once Lindsey got home, she slept in a way that she had never done. Maybe it was because of the new life forming inside of her, or perhaps it was the thought of disappointing her mother; whatever the case, she was exhausted. Her pastor did make that call to her mother, who was surprisingly calm about the situation. She would later learn that her mother had found a bill from her insurance company for one of her prenatal appointments. Netta's only concern was if and how/w Jaybone planned on taking care of Lindsey and their soon to be child. He thought about his father. Though he didn't live with his family, he was a dependable provider. He reassured her that he would be an honest man.

On October 23, 1992, Lindsey became the mother to a beautiful and healthy baby boy named Malik. The hospital waiting area was filled with family and friends as she gave birth to her son. Following her hospital stay, her and her new family stayed with her mother and her stepdad, Jeffery, with whom she had a hostile relationship. Jeffery was an abusive and intimidating man. But her mother adored him. Lindsey didn't trust him and made him aware of this any chance that she got. Being around him sullied her joy and shortened her stay.

Lindsey's new family was homeless. Her aunt Jo-Jo, a tall and graceful brown-skinned woman with a stoic expression and three children of her own allowed them to move in upstairs at her house. They carved out a beautiful space of their own in those tight quarters. The baby continued to grow healthily, and the two teenagers continued going to school and working their jobs. She was determined to graduate on time, and nothing was holding her back.

It was the night before graduation, and Jaybone, their friend, Mike, and Lindsey were in the basement "chilling". The boys started smoking weed and asked Lindsey if she wanted to hit it with them to celebrate. She declined, but they insisted because she was always taken as the prudish do-gooder that could afford to take it easy once in a while. She smoked the joint a few times and instantly got high; she laughed uncontrollably at nothing in particular, and so did they.

The next morning was the big day. The sun was beaming, the sky was clear, and the aroma of pride circulated the house. Lindsey was ready to defy the odds. Her house flooded with family ready for their darling to walk across that stage. She went to her purse to distribute the tickets, only to find that they were gone. Not one ticket in sight. She searched high and low, tearing up the room. Nothing. Her eyes began to well with tears as she panicked circulating the room as Jaybone sat there and watched her stoically. If she hadn't known any better, she we would have thought that he got some sort of kick at her anxiety. He wasn't graduating and told Lindsey he couldn't attend because he had to work.

"He took your tickets," said Aunt Jo-Jo.

"I felt that too," replied Lindsey.

"He's jealous that you're still graduating, and he's not." Lindsey's heart dropped because she knew that her aunt's words were true. Though painful, she wasn't going to let this ruin her day; so, they called Redford High and explained the situation. Lindsey was able to get more tickets, and her family was able to attend her graduation. That is when she began to know the Lord's favor.

Summer and fall came and went uneventfully with work, caretaking, planning, and a bit of fun in between. Winter was on the horizon as was true adulthood for Lindsey. It was time for her to come off of her mom's health insurance though neither her nor Jaybone's job offered it.

"You better go sign up for Medicaid and take care of your baby," Lindsey's aunt told her. Lindsey had no intentions of receiving public assistance because it required that the father be put on child support. However, because they didn't have the means to provide for Malik independently while paying for health insurance, she was left with little choice. Down to the Department of Human Services they went. Lindsey signed up for everything they offered, and her caseworker told her they had to establish paternity.

"Wait a minute. We signed papers at the hospital," Lindsey said.

"Well, it doesn't look like it," said the caseworker, "and in order for you to get any services, the father has to sign for paternity." Jaybone complied and signed the necessary paperwork. Shortly after that appointment, a thick book arrived at his house for child support payments. They both were angry because that was not how they saw the situation transpiring, but Jaybone's anger was hinted with bitterness. He believed that Lindsey was out to trap him.

"You know that's not what I wanted," she said. "We both were right there with the lady, and she didn't say anything about you being put on child support. I thought you were signing for the birth certificate." This situation opened up a new set of problems.

Chapter Two: The Dwelling Place

They finally moved into their first home as a family. Lindsey assumed her role as wife, though they were not legally married, beautifully. She cleaned. She cooked meals. She did laundry. She provided emotional support for Jaybone and Malik, and she worked. She had inherited these traits from her late grandmother who to her was the epitome of a devoted wife. But also like her grandmother, she had a smart mouth. If one was caught off guard, she could cut them with her words. With Jaybone she felt justified in her reactions based upon his actions. Though Lindsey was a devoted girlfriend, Jaybone assumed the role of taker. His friends would hang out at their house to drink and smoke weed, and he would stay out late, doing who knows what. They would get into arguments and fights about him staying out late and not responding to her pages, and when she learned that other girls were paging him; she would curse him out.

One day things had gotten so heated that Lindsey assaulted him, which turned into a physical fight. The police were called to the house and Jaybone was taken to jail. Before he got locked up that day, she had seen a text message from a girl and decided to play detective. Her friends would joke that she could have been an FBI agent because of her accuracy in catching Jaybone in a lie. Upon collecting data, she found the girl's address and rode past her house only to find out that she was living in Jaybone's old neighborhood. She confronted him and of course he fed her with lies, which led to another physical fight. While he was in jail, Lindsey had moved everything out of the house except for the refrigerator and a single white ice tray, and she and Malik went to live with her grandmother. One morning while getting him ready for school, he turned to her and said, "Don't cry momma, one day God is going to send you a man who's going to love and take care of you." He was only five. She stopped crying, gave him a hug, and they left for school.

That tiny spark reminded her that she was still loved despite the pain she had been suffering. She was going to need it too, because Jaybone had her ear again. He whipped out his charm and talked her into moving back in with him. They would send sexual messages, reminiscing on their most intimate moments, and she eventually let him court her again. The saw movies, went to expensive restaurants, and he would buy her gifts. It was back to the honeymoon phase, as she would come to call it; but that was only going to last for a while.

She had been dealing with hell back home, but her workplace offered her a much-needed respite. One day, doctor Rosenstein, the office's doctor-in-residence offered her a plate of baba ganoush, kugel, Israeli salad, and pita bread. He would often come in the office on Monday detailing his family's Shabbat happenings from Friday night and would sometimes rave about his wife's meals. She would sit and listen to his monologues if only to have a sample of his lunch. This time, after trying a few bites, she vomited the pasty mixture all over the office floor. This had never happened to her. For Lindsey, this could only mean one thing. She wiped the remnants from her mouth and headed straight to the bathroom to pee in one of the small, transparent cups that so many of her patients had used before. Some used them to test for STDs, some for other infections, and some used them to check their hCG levels. Lindsey anxiously awaited the results, which confirmed her suspicions. She was pregnant with her second child. Because she still had her menstrual cycle, and because she didn't know how far along she had been, she was told by the doctors to make an appointment immediately if she ever thought she was pregnant.

It was her first prenatal visit for her second baby. Before she went to her doctor's office, she used the bathroom, which was a regular occurrence. When she got up from the toilet, she found a white sac at the bottom of the porcelain bowl. She had known that pregnant women excreted a multitude of drainage, but this was strange. She called the doctor who told her to go to the emergency room immediately and to bring the sac in with her if she could. In tears, Lindsey called her mother-in-law Linda who came to take her to the emergency room. Jaybone didn't accompany them to the hospital, preferring to stay home with his friends and Malik. This only made matters worse for Lindsey. She felt devastated that he would rather stay with his friends instead of being with her through this crisis. Lindsey's face glistened with tears while Linda tried consoling her. She said to Lindsey, "I can't believe that he would stay home," and "you gotta stop all that crying Lindsey."

Once they got to the hospital and took Lindsey to the back, the doctor came in to examine her. The doctor informed her that there had been another sac.

"Where you having twins?"

Lindsey looked frantic and said, "I don't know, I had my first visit this week to find out everything."

"Well, based on your examination, I believe you were having twins."

"I'm so sorry, but we're going to have to do surgery because the baby is in your tubes, which is called an ectopic pregnancy. Were you not hurting anywhere because you're lucky it didn't rupture."

"No, not really. Only pressure in my bottom," Lindsey said.

As the tears rolled down her face, she cried, "I want my momma!" A nurse swiftly dialed her mother, and Lindsey explained what happened.

"Do you want me to come up there? I'll get on a plane and come," her mother said.

"That's ok momma, I just wish you were here with me." Her mother had moved to Knoxville, TN with her husband, Jeffery. Lindsey was not at all pleased with this decision given the history between her and her stepdad and his own violence directed at her mother. In her mind, he was creating distance between Netta and her family – a ploy to assault and belittle her in peace. They got off of the phone, and Lindsey was prepped for surgery, which went well, though she would be very fertile. It only took a few months for her to get pregnant again. This pregnancy proved to be significantly more difficult than the first. Her days were filled with nausea, vomiting, pain, and exhaustion. On one particular day, her pain and exhaustion took a turn for the worst. The typical pangs of pregnancy turned into excruciating throbs in her abdomen. When she started bleeding abnormally, she knew that it was time to visit the doctor. She was diagnosed with pelvic inflammatory disease, a sexually transmitted infection for which she was treated with IV antibiotics. She was livid. Curse words flew like rockets. Declarations of injustice like bombs. She knew that Jaybone had his share of affairs, but she didn't think he'd have the audacity to step outside of the relationship while she was pregnant. After the doctors told her what she had contracted, she cursed Jaybone out for not having enough respect for her to use protection while she was pregnant.

She put an end to their sexual relations. For the moment. She wanted to uphold this standard, but she knew Jaybone. He was unfaithful, and if he didn't get it from her, he'd get it from somewhere else; so, she continued to sleep with him, this time using protection. That condom wearing didn't last long, though. She stressed the issue of being pregnant and catching an STD, which could cause harm to their unborn child in hopes he wouldn't be a repeat offender. She frequently told him that they couldn't continue to live in sin even though she felt he was not the husband that God had for her. Somehow, she felt that God would do the changing if they did the right thing.

"Are you ready to go get married?" Lindsey woke up to the sun sparkling through the window of their first home in the middle of September on a beautiful Friday morning. She was two months into her pregnancy, and Jaybone woke her up to these words. These words that she had been praying for him to ask. Even after the marriage counseling with her Pastor and Elder, who recommended that they wait because of the unhealthy baggage they would bring into the marriage, they still went and got married. Lindsey got her hair done. Jaybone got his haircut. They headed to Lucas, Ohio where the process was simple. He rolled his joint and then stopped at KFC to get a two piece and a biscuit. It was lunchtime, and the highway was a sea of cars, which made them late. Ten minutes too late. The marriage office was closed. September 15, 1997, was the day they missed getting married.

"Don't tell anybody we didn't get married. We'll just come back Monday," Jaybone said. Though somewhat disappointed, Lindsey considered this to be God telling them that marriage was not in their best interest. Still, she thought it better than simply "shacking up"; so, she did it anyway. When they returned home, they were met with reassuring smiles and heartfelt congratulations. Unfortunately, her conviction wasn't as strong as their good wishes as she did not like to lie. Still, she forced a smile and hugged her family, receiving their support.

Over the weekend, Jaybone lost his driver's license. Before leaving a convenience store, he had been looking for his wallet, which he had often misplaced. That next Monday, he went to apply for a new one but had to wait six weeks for it to come in the mail since at that time one could only get a paper license with a picture. She looked at this as another sign that they should not be getting married; but again, she ignored it.

On November 12, 1997, Jaybone and Lindsey got married. This was not how Lindsey pictured it, standing in the hallway of a courthouse saying vows surrounded by a bunch of people who looked like they had just woken up or gotten off of work. She wanted to be in a church surrounded by family and friends and in the presence of the Lord.

Six months later, on May 19, 1998, they welcomed another beautiful baby boy and moved into a townhouse. It was a medium-sized, two-story lair with two bedrooms and a basement off of Chicago, a busy street on the westside of Detroit. She was a young wife, mother of two boys, working a part-time job, and going to cosmetology school. On the other hand, Jaybone worked for a construction company and made a little extra money on the side selling drugs. She would often help him by securing customers from her school. One of her classmates, who had also been a customer, offered her a ride home from school one day. She was hesitant at first in order to avoid Jaybone's rage, but because he had been on her feet all day, and because her legs could not take waiting for a bus that would often come late; she took the ride. Accusations flew of her and the guy messing around, and she was told that she could never ride with him or any other man again. The next week, she received a call from the health department. She had contracted gonorrhea.

"Wait a minute," she said, "ya'll must have made a mistake because I just had my pap smear, and I also regularly get tested for STDs. My doctor's office called me and said all of my tests were normal."

"Well, we received your name so you have to come in," the administrator said.

"No, this is wrong. I don't have anything."

"We need to recheck you and treat you and your partner." She slammed down the phone and questioned Jaybone about this new development.

"I ain't been with nobody," he said calmly. *A lie*. "It must've been you and that nigga who dropped you off."

"I ain't been with nobody and you know that!" She said through screams and yells, tears and agony. Though she was hysterical, she was also dumbfounded. Her tests came back normal. She called her doctor's office to verify her results; and again, they were normal. They went down to the health department and checked-in. As the nurse examined them, his test came back negative. Lindsey's heart began to beat, her brain was in knots, and her shoulders were tense. She felt like she could explode. Her throat clenched and her chest was a heavy lump. What was happening? Was she going insane? She was Lindsey. Devoted, faithful, and loyal despite it all. She couldn't imagine being with anyone else. After Jaybone's examination came Lindsey's. She tested positive for gonorrhea.

"How could this be? My doctors said all of my tests were negative. I just don't understand this!"

The nurse replied, "either he had gotten treated already and didn't tell you, or it laid dormant and too far up in him that he didn't have any symptoms."

"Yeah, he had to get treated, because this is crazy. I have not been with anybody but my husband."

Jaybone remained calm and unflinching throughout that whole ordeal while Lindsey oscillated between rage and deep sadness culminating in tear-stained cheeks and swollen eyelids. They got treated and left.

Lindsey's mind continued to spiral in a ball of confusion, self-doubt swimming like minnows in the sea. Jaybone, on the other hand, remained at ease. Was he enjoying her anguish? She kept saying, "I know I didn't sleep with nobody. This is crazy." She cried so much that day until she left the house walking wherever her feet took her. She bought a bottle of Cisco and a pack of cigarettes although she hated the cancer sticks and took a drink every now and then. She cried and walked, she cried and smoked, she cried and drank until she found herself back home sleeping that horrible day off.

She finally graduated from Cosmetology school, and he attended her graduation with the rest of her family. That night, her and Jaybone danced in unison, both on the dance floor and with the love that flowed between them. In that moment, the pains of yesterday melted away. They were back in a honeymoon period, which seemed to be a theme in their relationship.

After the graduation festivities ended, she went to Knoxville, Tennessee to visit her mother and Jeffery. She enjoyed the visit so much that she decided to move her family there. She figured a new state might fill the turbulent voids in their marriage. *Boy was she wrong.*

Chapter Three: Wrong Turn

It was Halloween, and the fall trees had emptied their leaves. Jaybone and Lindsey were getting adjusted to their new town. It had been their first time moving away from home, but they'd been optimistic about the change. Jeffrey drove up to Detroit to move them down to Knoxville, and Lindsey immediately sought employment. Always a hard-worker, she found employment at both Brothers and Sisters hair salon and RHA health services. Jaybone hadn't moved down yet; he had gone back to Detroit to finish "taking care of business". His drug-dealing had surmounted. A quick deal here and there turned into lugging ounces of weed, crack, and cocaine from Detroit to Knoxville in his Caprice classic. Sometimes these trips would include a clandestine affair or three. When he finally came to Knoxville to stay, he found a job at Ameristeel, a local steel company. Though money was coming in and their home situation was reasonably peaceful, she still cried everyday, desperately missing her family and friends. Her mother reassured her that it would get better as she had gone through a similar situation. But it had only gotten worse. He began to meet people through Jeffrey's relatives. On top of that, he left his job at Ameristeel because someone had "disrespected him". He decided to work at RHA with Lindsey.

They finally moved into their own house, which is when things truly started to take a fall. What's worse is that she would often receive backlash from his friend's. They considered her to be mean and attitudinal just for standing up to his despicable behavior. At this point, he was getting even more immersed into the street life, and with the street life came *women*. His interactions with these women was a bitter cocktail of business and pleasure, though he would often deny any ill-intentions.

Girls would call his phone day and night for a "sell", and she would see nude pictures and obscene messages, which always led to another fight. More than that, he would be out late at night while she worked overnight at her 2nd job. Fighting and making up was their troubled dance and would become the norm for their marriage. He would cheat and she'd retaliate with rage, but still she took him back because he took care of his responsibilities as a father, and he in turn had no reason to believe that she would ever leave him. After each tryst, he would shower her with his dreams and desires for them – their large home, their vintage cars, their wealthy lifestyle. He'd also shower Lindsey with expensive gifts and fund her personal care. Anything to make her stay and rebuild her faith in him.

"I'm going to kill him! I'm going to kill him!" Cried a hysterical Lindsey. It was a bitter and cool night, an anomaly for Knoxville, which was known for its muggy days and humid evenings. Jaybone and Lindsey were on their way back home when Lindsey seeped into a rage, the tension of her hatred towards her stepfather, her homesickness, and her resentment towards Jaybone rose to a boiling point. Not only had Jaybone and she been arguing the entire ride home, she had recently had an argument with Jeffery, which meant that she was all but banned from her mother's house. Even though her mother often visited Jaybone's and her home attempting to keep the peace, it still wasn't enough. Although she had moved to Knoxville to be closer to her mother, she started to regret her decision to leave Detroit; at least there she had loved ones for whom she could rely. She was simply broken-hearted, overstressed, and insanely sad. As they were driving, still arguing, Lindsey started to experience a feeling that she didn't understand. She was out of control.

"What the hell are you doing?!!" Lindsey flung Jaybone's car door open and began sprinting down the street on foot. She was headed to Netta's house, hell-bent on killing Jeffery with her bare hands.

She ended up at a local store still screaming, "I'm going to kill him!" while onlookers stood by dumbfounded. Her hands were shaking as she mustered the courage to dial 911. Her breathing was shallow and quivering as she told the operator that she was about to kill someone.

Lindsey's mind was a haze as the operator began asking her questions. Questions about her mental state. Questions about her location. Questions about her plan. Lindsey couldn't remember anything. Finally, an officer arrived, and they called an ambulance to pick her up. She was taken to the hospital where they couldn't calm her down, so instead she was transferred to a psychiatric state hospital. She was irate and hysterical as two steely armed men and a surly woman held her down and strapped her to the bed. They warned her about the consequences she'd face if she didn't calm down. *How did I get in this situation?* was the only thought that she could muster. A once honor roll student, apple of her family's eye, church-going virgin was now decreased to lying on a hard surface in a cold place restrained like some animal. After several more attempts, she finally calmed down and was later sent to a room with women only. Because it was a Friday, she had to wait until Monday to see a doctor. She laid in the bed and cried all night. Then suddenly, when she thought He had forgotten her, she heard the voice of the Lord telling her to let it go and forgive, or death would take her.

"Ma, are the boys okay?" That morning she called her mom who had stayed with her children during her time in the hospital. In that moment, Lindsey became a child again. Only wanting her mother. Only needing her mother. "And mom, I don't want to talk to Jaybone, but if you want, you can tell him where I am." She hung up the phone and went back to sit with the women who would become her tribe while she healed. She tried her best to feel like a person in the translucent gown and fluffy yellow socks. She glided the floor like the queen of the pack. She held mini Bible studies and prayer sessions in the terribly lit common area. The women sat intently while Lindsey began praying for them and talking to them about the Lord. She was offered medication and therapy, but this was the real healing that she needed. As she poured into these women, God poured into her, and she started to feel a release. That night, she prayed and asked God to forgive her, and she rested peacefully. On Sunday morning, she called her mom and asked to speak to her step-dad. She told him that she forgave him and that she loved him. He told her that he loved her too; the burden had finally lifted.

"I don't ever want to see you in a place like this again." Lindsey's doctor said. He was a tall, sweet-faced man who wore thin-rimmed glasses and a blue suit under his white coat. "You don't belong here," he said. "I believe you were just extremely stressed. But next time, if you find yourself in a place like this, go to your church and talk to your pastor. Just don't come here." The doctor agreed to release her under the condition that she'd promise to never come back. That was no tall order for Lindsey who had already made it up in her mind that she'd lean on God during those tough times instead of on her own devices.

Not too soon after her hospital stay and weeks after looking for the perfect church home for her family, another test of faith surfaced. Unlike the photos where mothers held their beautiful babies, staring lovingly into their eyes with a rainbow in the rear; Lindsey was bitter, lonely, and deeply depressed. In between appointments and pregnancy pains, she spent most of her days in bed crying herself to sleep. Her pregnancy was miserable. She abhorred every moment of it.

"Why don't you just have an abortion cus you gonna mess my baby up with all that crying." A fed up Jaybone exclaimed to her on one particularly difficult day. Throughout her pregnancy, he once again reared his ugly head. He demeaned her while spending more days and nights in the streets instead of coddling her throughout this difficult time.

Despite it all, she delivered a beautiful, healthy, 10lbs and 3oz baby girl with a sweet face and a dimple to match. As beautiful as she was though, that did not stop Lindsey from planning for ways to escape her dysfunctional marriage. Her beauty also did not help to assuage her difficulty with bonding with Jada. Each day she did the minimal to care for her baby girl and two boys, finding herself mostly in bed.

Days turned into weeks, and Lindsey eventually dug herself out of her desperate depression through radically petitioning God as well as help from seasoned saints. Sometimes as a family they went to church and of course those would be the good days, or the honeymoon period, until a random female would call; and the honeymoon period was over.

One particular girl was Scarlet. A thick-bodied, dark-haired white woman who looked about half Jaybone's age. The consensus between he and his friends, all years away from maturity, was that white women were passive; that they would let him get away with anything, and scoring one with curves was the ultimate success.

It had been another night of Jaybone ignoring Lindsey's calls and attempting to hide this fact with a blanket of pathetic lies. This particular night his lies had been so absurd that she drove to an apartment complex, confident that he was there, and knocked on four doors until he popped out of the proverbial box. Instead of finding Jaybone, Shayna, Scarlet's sister peeked out of one of those doors. She was a loyal sister. Lindsey wrapped her fingers around the thick wooden door, but Shayna hurriedly closed it in her face. Unfortunately, sister wasn't strong enough, because Lindsey pushed the door open and rammed into the house.

"Were they at!" she exclaimed as she searched the apartment like a narc pursuing a raid.

"Get the hell out!" Shayna yelled, but it was pointless, Lindsey continued to stomp through the house until she reached the closed door that held Jaybone and

Scarlet. Lindsey tried to open the door, but Jaybone had pressed his entire weight against it. His lies, his betrayal, his selfishness, a boulder against her weakened body. Scarlet would have been easy to take down, but not Jaybone. She stood no chance against the power of his will, so she relented and went back home. When he finally returned to their shattered nest, a place where she oddly had enough power to argue, they fought all night; and she cried herself to sleep.

It was pitch black in that house. The darkness of the outside was a reflection of their world. Lindsey woke up in the middle of the night to an empty bed. Her fingers moved rapidly as she dialed his number once, twice, ten times, to no answer. She finally texted him a string of curse words and ultimatums, which led him home. She was tired and vulnerable, but she couldn't bare another affair. She hovered over him, hoping to ignite his passion.

Instead of sinking into the sheets, letting her love cover his, he put up a struggle. Not a violent one but a stiff arm so full of rejection that Lindsey could faint. Exhausted with embarrassment, Lindsey retreated and Jaybone went to sleep. Though she had been rejected, she wasn't stupid. As Jaybone lay there, snoring like a satisfied lion, she went through his phone and wallet and found the evidence that solidified her suspicions. In between his ID and credit card was a slender hotel key nestled inside a small white envelope. She called the hotel to see if the room was in his name. It was. She quickly got dressed and drove the fifteen miles to the hotel. Once there, she went to every room until the thin key signaled a green light on the dingy hotel door. "You f!@#$%* my husband b*@#%!" She didn't wait for a response; instead she allowed her rage, her despair, and her fists do the talking for her. After rounds of fist pounding, Lindsey finally peeled herself off of Willow, a mutual friend of theirs, who had cowered like a meek lamb.

"NO, NO, I was with MJ, I wasn't with Jaybone, we just friends."

"Why my husband got y'all hotel card in his wallet?" Lindsey was a wolf. She did not care that her and Willow were both women. They were two women pulled in multiple directions by the same puppet master.

"He got the room for us." Willow said with desperation.

"Girl, you must think I'm a fool!" Lindsey said. Lindsey made Willow call Jaybone on the phone, and when he answered her call, Lindsey snatched the phone and cursed him out. His nose must have grown inches with the lies that spurted out of his mouth. Lindsey was still furious, a tasmanian devil in a desert storm.

"Give me the money you owe my cousin!" Lindsey shouted. Willow had owed Lindsey's cousin money for doing her hair. They had been good friends. Willow had joined Linsey on trips back home to Detroit, and she had introduced her to family.

"I don't have any money to give." Willow said.

"Oh, so you laying up with a nigga for free. You stupid." Lindsey left and went home, and of course, it was a disaster when she arrived.

Their wedding anniversary approached, and she prepared a night for them after she had gotten off of work. She cooked a festive medley of their favorite seafood, dressed their bed in satin sheets, and filled the house with romantic music, jazz and R&B classics. Jaybone showed his anticipation, but had to deliver drugs to a customer before they spent their night together. He kissed her cheek and left home, promising that he'd be back soon.

It was getting late. His "quick run" had turned into all night and led to more unanswered phone calls, more reasons to fight. Because it was their anniversary though, Lindsey gave him the benefit of the doubt. Surely he would not step out of their marriage on their anniversary. She called the local hospitals and jail to see if they had him. She drove around some areas where he might've been, but he was nowhere to be found. After a night of fruitless searching, she went back home and fell asleep after taking care of Jada and preparing for the boys' school day. Dawn was approaching, and the door creaked open, Jaybone's footsteps like an offbeat drum in Lindsey's tired ears, which aroused her. She didn't say a word as he walked up the stairs; she only grabbed her gun, pointed it in his direction, and pulled the trigger. She missed him by only an inch.

As her outerworld was one of torment and unrelenting violence, her innerworld was considerably worse. Guilt and shame ate her alive. Her dreams slowly turned into euphoric fantasies about ending her life. Jaybone came home one day and found her in the bathroom on the floor crying with an empty pill bottle lying beside her and blood running down her wrist. He frantically called Netta and told her what had happened. Nearly losing her breath, she pleaded for Jaybone to give Lindsey the phone. Lindsey refused. She didn't want to feel better. She didn't want comfort. She wanted Jaybone to see what he had reduced her to. Her prayer book was replaced with a gun, her soul a vacant space with no room even for God.

Chapter Four: The Plea

"I slipped on a patch of ice." She looked up at her doctor as he sutured the bloody gnash in the top of her head. Jaybone had caught her calling Scarlet in the parking lot of the hair salon where she worked, searching for answers, an explanation, anything to keep her away from her husband. Because of this, she paid a sore price; she suffered a blow to the head with his loaded gun. Her appointment book was filled with a load of eager clients, yet Lindsey spent her day at the hospital, lying to a concerned doctor. She was sent home as the gnash was painful enough for her to need stitches but tolerable enough for her to go on about her life. This was not too different from what she had endured in her relationship with Jaybone. He pushed her far away enough to leave space for his escapades while keeping her close enough to abuse and manipulate her. And that he did. After she returned home, he didn't apologize; instead, he blamed her for his loss of control. And still there were more girls, but Lindsey never starved for affection. When he was with her, he was courting his wife. He would make love to her daily, and have an affair weekly. When he wasn't making love to her, he was blaming her for his indiscretions If only she did what other women allowed him to do, he'd have no reason to stray.

As their marriage progressed, his affairs grew more careless. One girl in particular left evidence at their door of her and him together. On their porch lay a bag with a chalet receipt, an empty bottle of wine, and a shirt. She took it to him and immediately punched him in his head, provoking another physical fight. It wasn't him he had said. It was her and his friend he told her. He jumped in the car and went to the mystery woman's house to question her about coming to he and Lindsey's home. But there was no use; Lindsey had also read text messages with sweet nothings and thank yous for him paying for her hair appointment.

The girl's name was Lilith. Another white girl, as if he had some sort of fetish. For a long time, Lindsey thought that Lilith was a black girl, she had a familiar tone and way of speaking. Lilith quickly debunked this assumption, describing herself as a thick white girl who "didn't take no mess." She had a thing for black guys and was the type of girl who Lindsey *might* have befriended had she not been screwing her husband. It had been another night of unreturned phone calls and ignored text messages, so Lindsey hopped in their old, rigged car and followed her intuition right into Lilith's home. When she got to the house, the door was unlocked, so she helped herself inside. The lights were out, the TV was on, and there were kids sleeping on the couch. She knew he was there. Not only was her truck parked outside of the shabby brick home, but she could smell his stench. She paced the entire house until she found two unlocked doors. She chose the door on the right and Jaybone was sitting on the bed with his pants down while Lilith sprang up off of the floor. As Jaybone struggled to pull his pants up, Lindsey and Lilith exchanged fists and hair pulls and unrelenting scratches. Her rage was at a boiling point. Once Jaybone had pried her off of Lilith, Lindsey turned those same punches onto him. This time he didn't fight back. "It's dark out. Let's take this home." She didn't care. She had already been embarrassed beyond repair. Why not get revenge too? Once they got home, she called one of Jaybone's older brothers and told him what had transpired.

"Why you don't leave my brother? You don't deserve to go through all this stuff he's been putting you through."

"I don't have the strength," she said. She knew deep down inside this was not the life she wanted to live or die in, even after praying that things would change; in her heart, she knew they wouldn't. They were unequally yoked.

It was mega millions season and the lottery had just been released in Tennessee. Lindsey was checking out at the gas station, when she heard, "are you going to get one of those tickets?"

"Nope, the lottery is not new to me. I'm from Detroit, we already had the lottery." He was a caramel-skinned man with a charming smile and sturdy demeanor. Lindsey had been a faithful, devoted wife in her farce of a marriage, but had grown weary with Jaybone's tormenting abuse and egregious extramarital affairs; so, she decided to get even. She felt pangs of guilt as he was also married, but she couldn't resist; and the fact that he wore a uniform – he was a police officer – didn't hurt either.

"Oh Detroit? What brings you down here to Knoxville?"

"I followed my momma." Lindsey replied while paying for her favorite evening snack.

"You got a minute?" *No, I have a husband. A psychotic, abusive, controlling husband she was thinking.*

"Yeah," She hesitantly replied. They sat in the store and talked for over an hour about everything and nothing while she periodically looked over her shoulder for Jaybone. In her eyes, this would certainly be the day she died had he caught her entertaining another man. It was getting late and she told him she had to go home. He asked for her number, and she said, "Give me your number, I'll call you." For a moment she felt like a woman again. She was being pursued, flattered, even a bit adored. She waited a few days before calling him and was surprised when their innocent little chat outside of a poorly lit gas station turned into frequent late-night telephone calls, which she enjoyed more than she could ever admit.

"Someone is up front to see you." Her co-worker Lisa said with a half-smile. She figured that it was her husband, but from Lisa's adoring blush, she couldn't help but second guess this assumption. It was Brice, the handsome police officer.

"What are you doing here, and how did you find out where I worked?" She said half confused and half elated.

"I got my ways," he said with a smile. *Well, he is a police officer.* She was a nervous wreck as they walked outside, hoping that Jaybone didn't pop up. He never even noticed her shaking, too lost in her eyes, too comforted in their easy conversation. She had been gone for a while, and it was time for her to get back to work. They walked to the hospital's parking garage where he hugged her and planted a single, gentle but passionate, kiss on her quivering lips. She felt thrilled and terrible at the same time. *I'm going to hell* she thought while walking back to the office. Time passed, and he suggested that they take their little affair further. He shared how unhappy he was in his marriage, and she shared the despair she suffered by being with Jaybone. Still, she was not ready to commit adultery. Even though Jaybone had disrespected their marriage in every way one could imagine, her main loyalty was to God; and for her this meant being faithful to her husband. She made all kinds of excuses not to meet up with him, but one day temptation got the best of her; and she decided that she wanted to find out what it'd be like to share herself with another man. They would stay up late night having intimate conversations, exploring each other's minds and discussing their sexual desires. *This is all wrong,* she thought. When their conversations led down a road to which they couldn't recover, she hesitantly told him, "We're both married, "and lessened her contact with him before eventually cutting him off completely. Even though she didn't go all of the way with him, she still wanted Jaybone to feel some of her pain.

    She shared tales of her little love affair with their mutual friend, Willow, the same girl that Jaybone was suspected of messing around with. This was not a friendly exchange between two girlfriends, though, her only intention was for Willow to run and tell Jaybone, which she did; and he was livid! She wiggled out of it by telling Jaybone that Willow had been lying; but the look on his face, the pain that he had shown, was a sweet revenge that made her feel empowered, if only for a little while.

Their marriage continued to be wrought with strife as one issue after another arose with Lindsey plotting her escape. What she thought was the last incident turned out to be a springboard for a phone call that nearly broke her.

One day, out of the blue, she received a phone call from a woman who claimed that Jaybone had fathered her child. It turned out to be a lie – this girl only wanted money; and Lindsey could breathe, dodging the bullet of an illegitimate child. On another occasion, Lindsey read a text message in Jaybone's phone, detailing that the woman was pregnant. She called the woman and gave her all of the details about her and Jaybone's relationship. Jaybone had told this woman that Lindsey was his sister and that he only had two children. "Well no, he is married with three kids and I'm not his sister," Lindsey snapped.

She said that she would not keep the baby, and Lindsey told her they would pay for the abortion. When Lindsey confronted Jaybone with the news, he denied that he was the father.

Lindsey kept her word, and her and the woman scheduled an appointment for an abortion at 1:30pm on a Tuesday. Lindsey stood in the parking lot of the clinic under greyish clouds and checked her phone by the minute. Her screen remained black, and her heart was slowly sinking. She decided to go inside. *Maybe she was already there. Maybe she was early.* She searched the waiting room for a woman with a red shirt and black jeans. She wasn't there. The woman never showed up, and Lindsey never heard from her again. Her sinking heart cracked as she walked back to her car embarrassed, ashamed, and angry.

Sadly, she wasn't in the clear. Just months after the abortion center incident, she received a phone call from another woman relaying that Jaybone had gotten someone pregnant. This time it was true. Their jaded cycle continued as Lindsey found herself in the same predicament that inspired a humiliation of which she had never knew existed. This girl was 17 years old. Three years older than Malik. Jaybone once again denied that he was the father, but the dates were adding up. She started to feel as if she were a guest on the Maury Povich show. Deep down Lindsey felt that Jaybone fathered this baby.

Malik and this teenager were zoned for the same high school, which added to her embarrassment. *How could she send her son to school with a girl that his father had impregnated*? She had made up her mind that they would move to Atlanta. Atlanta would give them a fresh start; their former life would be a faint mist outlining the Smoky Mountains.

Before they headed southward though, Lindsey had to make one stop. She met with the young girl's foster parents at their home. They apologized profusely while praying fervently that Jaybone did not get their baby girl pregnant. "We told her that, that man was married with a family just from the things she would tell us," the girl's mother said through sporadic tears. She was a kind, middle-aged woman with a home that smelled like peppermint and leftover Thanksgiving Dinner. The father sat in his Lazy-Boy chair silently processing what could be the beginning of an uphill future. "You're such a beautiful young lady, and we hate this has happened to you." She composed herself and gave Lindsey a comforting hug, a mother's hug that whispered, "we're in this together." They told her they would keep in touch, and Lindsey left with a heavy heart but also with an odd sense of relief. Jaybone never knew Lindsey met with the girl's foster parents. The reality of this matter made her decision to move easier.

She started making phone calls to Jaybone's family in Atlanta about employment in which they would live. In between school drop-offs and pick-ups, work, and avoiding more of Jaybone's drama, Netta, the kids, and Lindsey would drive to Atlanta on the weekends and look for houses. Everything was coming together as planned, and Lindsey secured the house that she wanted. She still hadn't found a job but continued to search for one.

The night before they got ready to move, Lindsey wrote all of their hurts on a piece of paper and stood in front of a red-orange fire. They were going to fold up those hurts and toss them in, in hopes that the blaze would burn up their past. They both held the paper as he lit it, and she said a prayer for new beginnings. They hugged and kissed and walked away from the pit. Though she prayed that this move would be the new start that they so desperately needed, she never prayed if it was God's will for them to move. On July 15, 2006, they said goodbye to Knoxville, TN and hello to College Park, GA.

PART II: For the Necessary is Now

Chapter Five: The Turnaround

College Park was a quaint suburb just outside of Atlanta with a railroad track running through its downtown, giving the place a historic feel with an artsy, modern touch - a colorful mural painted on an aging building being a stand-out feature. Evergreens and magnolias shade its neatly sewn parks, and the liberal, smiling residents made Lindsey feel at ease. It was cozy and homey and had also birthed an impressive list of prolific rap artists, a feature that her two boys would surely come to love.

The three-hour drive felt like a decade to the Wises, who were brimming with childlike anticipation to start their new life. The air felt delicate on their skin, almost dissolving the nicks and bruises they'd endured in

Knoxville. The sun was a bit hotter in Georgia, but it would grow on them. They were just happy to be in a new city, with new people, and a new peace of mind. They had stayed in a hotel for a week until their house was ready but had found some favorite spots that made them feel at home.

It was the beginning of August when they arrived; the kids were enrolled in school, but Jaybone hadn't landed a job; so not too long after they had gotten settled, he was driving back and forth up the highway making runs until he found steadier work. Lindsey too had loose ends to tie up back in Knoxville. Paperwork had to be signed, belongings had to be stored, and appointments had to be honored. While getting gas during one particular trip back from Knoxville, Lindsey saw the woman who had left the empty champagne bottle and chalet receipt on her doorstep. Her new beginning couldn't save this woman as she got out of their van, walked into the store, and without saying a word, punched the poor girl in the face. Fur flew as the two women tore up the store. The rumble nearly looked even until Lindsey pinned her to the ground and spat, "I told you I was gonna get you b!@#%!," and walked back out of the store. As she got closer to the van, Malik jumped out, a hero going to rescue his mother. But she didn't need it. She promptly told him to sit back in his seat, and they headed back to College Park as if nothing had happened.

When they got back to Atlanta, she continued applying to various hospitals and doctors' offices to no avail. She was becoming a bit discouraged until she noticed a hair salon with a booth rental sign in the window. She had gone out to shop at Wal-Mart and walked into a new opportunity. The salon owner liked her immediately and offered her a booth after one phone call.

Lindsey was reluctant to give it a try because she didn't have any clientele. A couple of months had passed, and she received a call from the owner, asking if she was still interested in the gig. Lindsey reminded her that she was new to the city and didn't have clientele, but she would give it a try. The owner offered her one week free and charged $200 a week for both rent thereafter. "Ok Lord, if this is what you have for me, then I'm going to need you to send the people," she prayed. She started at the salon the following Monday to a long line of customers whom she studied nervously. She had been doing hair since she was a little girl, apprenticing for her aunt Jo-Jo; but that didn't stop the butterflies doing cartwheels in her stomach. She was the new kid in the booth, after all. After the first client, she fell into a groove, and that week she made $850 off of walk-ins alone. With this new momentum, she was ready to build a clientele. She recruited her children to join her in marketing her growing business, spending their afternoons doing homework and passing out flyers in any direction that looked profitable. From that week forward, her clientele grew like wild flowers. Some of the other stylists in the salon were amazed at how quickly she had gotten clientele, commenting on how her spirit brought such a different atmosphere to the place.

    Her work life was going well, her home life was relatively stable, but she didn't feel complete without a church home. One day, while giving her client, San, a ride home, they began conversing about church. They barely noticed the streets passing being so engulfed in sharing stories of how they loved praising and worshipping their Creator on Sunday. As they pulled up to her home, San invited Lindsey to her church, Higher Ground Church of God and Christ. It was a small church with a family feel and an upbeat and down to Earth crowd. After one Sunday of fellowship, prayer, and receiving a penetrating word, Lindsey shared how she would certainly be back to visit. Her children and she even raved about their experiences to Jaybone, who would join them from time to time. Lindsey knew this was the church for them but was not ready to commit. Once she made that commitment, she knew there was no "playing church" this time, no more straddling the fence. Plus, she was still making drug runs with her husband, and she would at times make solo runs when he was out of town. In her mind they were partners; and he made sure to remind her of this fact by sharing how his friends' girls were "down" with them, which made her feel guilty if she didn't follow suit. He'd also pressured her into smoking weed by that same logic. Other girls were smoking with him, and if she loved him, she would do it too. He'd ease her anxiety by telling her what kind of weed they were smoking, and if it was the "good stuff", she'd agree to partake. One time while serving a customer weed and cocaine in Knoxville, Jaybone offered her a blunt. "This that homegrown good stuff, the best; you wanna hit it with me?" She agreed and felt blissfully intoxicated after just a few hits. This feeling was unique from any other weed that he had given her. She felt as if she were floating on air; her body was tingling all over, and she liked it.

She continued to go along with his schemes even though she felt unsettled; both because she truly wanted to commit her life to God and also because she did not approve of her husband's business sense, or lack thereof. Not only did he often cut his customers slack when they didn't have enough money, but he would also indulge in his own supply. "How do you expect to make money if you always want to give a deal and smoke the product?" she asked him. "That's why this is not for you. You need to get a job." That conversation opened up a turbulent argument as he blamed her for his lack of employment, bringing up both his child support payments and the fees he had to pay for the case he caught from a shoot-out they were both involved in.

This still didn't alter Lindsey's conviction. She became increasingly involved in the church; she mailed in her tithes when she couldn't make it, and she also accepted a challenge by her first lady to sacrifice her late hair clients in order to attend Bible study. "If you sacrifice your appointment times to not miss bible study, I promise God will make it so you won't miss a dollar," Lady Jones had said. The Lord fulfilled this promise, and she didn't miss a dollar, nor did she have to work harder to make up for it.

Though her prayers for abundance kept money in her pocket, she continued to endure problems on the home front. One night after coming home from Bible study, she opened her phone to a picture of a beautiful baby boy who resembled Jaybone. The teenage girl's foster parents had sent Lindsey a picture of their grandson. What she felt in her heart was true; the baby was indeed her husband's.

Lindsey had grown up in a solid church-going family who felt only through prayer and supplication could real changes occur in their lives. Around Thanksgiving meals or special family occasions they'd hold hands while giving thanks to God between jubilating cries of "hallelujah!" and "amen!" Lindsey and her cousins, being just babes, had their little prayers too. As they looked around at the adults, stomachs growling with hunger, wondering when it'd all be over, they would sometimes be summoned to offer a prayer or scripture as well. So, in order to get to the aromatic feast, they'd often recite the powerful and pithy,

"Jesus wept". Because her savior did, this gave Lindsey permission to do the same in her predicament. When she opened up that text message and saw Jaybone's love child, she cried like a river; and through sobs and a broken heart, she still managed to muster, "we can get through this." She felt sorry for the baby boy because of his living situation and told her husband that they could get custody of him and raise him. She began to feel love for him as if he were her own, which in her mind he was, simply because he was a part of her husband. As Lindsey's heart bristled with compassion, Jaybone's was full of deceit. He would deny his fatherhood while stealthily meeting the baby's needs. Lindsey would find receipts lined with lists of pacifiers, diapers, clothes, and other baby items.

It was a Sunday morning and Lindsey didn't go to church. She had fallen into a heavy depression. Instead of putting on nude stockings and sensible pumps, she threw on a hoodie and oversized pants and drove around until she found a dead-end street. Still weeping, she sent a picture of herself to selected family and friends telling them that she was about to kill herself. She sat in the car with her gun in her hand, eyes stinging with tears, petitioning God. For the first time in a long time, she was angry with Him. She felt an unrelenting, painful anger that penetrated through her entire being. "Whyyyy? Why is this happening to me God?! God, why are you hurting me like this?! JUST LET ME DIE!" As she raised the loaded gun to her head, her children flashed before her eyes, and she couldn't bring herself to pull the trigger. She ignored all of the panicked calls and texts she received, including those from Jaybone and the kids begging her to please come home. Jaybone filled her inbox with remorseful texts and a storm of apologies. Lindsey's heart rate had finally fallen and her breathing steadied. Her body was still exhausted from tears, but her budding headache was intensified by the dinging notifications of her phone; so, she finally responded to him telling him that she couldn't take it anymore and that she wanted a divorce. He apologized for everything and told her that he'd do whatever it took to win her back. Of course, she went back home, and they talked things over.

"It's about time." First Lady Jones smiled as she took Jaybone's hands in hers and opened the doors of Higher Ground Church of God in Christ to him and his family. They were officially members. No more straddling the fence. No more playing Christian. Though she did have some doubts, Lindsey was still overjoyed, believing that her prayers were finally being answered. A couple of Sundays after joining, Lindsey scheduled a meeting with Pastor and First Lady Jones to discuss their marriage. "We are here to help y'all," they assured them. "Y'all are going to be alright. Y'all will get through this." This gave them hope that their marriage could be salvaged after all. Jaybone started coming to Sunday school, Bible class, and Sunday service more, his interest in church seemingly authentic. He had also found work. Pastor Jones had given him a tile job to complete; and from there, word spread of his expertise, providing him with more job opportunities. Jaybone had learned the trade from his father and Lindsey tried convincing him to go into business for himself. She had business cards made for him and would sing his praises every chance she got. She believed in him and she knew he could run his own business as he had gotten pretty adept at conducting street business. His dealing had fully funded their lifestyle with Lindsey's income serving as a supplement. Once again, things were looking up; he had even seemed to relinquish his bachelor lifestyle. Whereas Lindsey would once spend her nights worrying where he was and with whom; now, she knew. He was right beside her, in bed, reading his Bible. Lindsey had joined the choir and was also asked to join the praise team. It had all seemed too good to be true when Pastore Jones approached Jaybone and asked him to be a deacon. Indeed, God had heard her prayers, *or so she thought.*

Chapter Six: Unexplainable Moves of Faith

"This ain't enough money," hissed Jaybone. It didn't take long before he sabotaged his job working at the minister's house, believing that he had been underpaying him. What started out as a simple annoyance turned into full blown animosity, resulting in Jaybone cursing him out and threatening his life. Being the man that he was, Pastor Jones attempted to diffuse the situation, using every tool in his arsenal to calm Jaybone down because he had been passionate about providing Jaybone with employment.

Shortly after that incident, though, Jaybone got into another argument with two guys from the church he had been working with. His reason was that they didn't pay him enough money. He eventually quit. Soon enough, he fell back onto what was familiar, selling drugs.

Though Lindsey stayed faithful to her calling in the ministry, she still accompanied Jaybone on some of his runs. On one return trip from Florida, he got mad at a gas station cashier and cursed her out. Lindsey couldn't help but be embarrassed. As they were coming out of the store, a passerby tried and failed to talk sensibly to him. "I am a pastor," he said.

"Yeah? Well, I'm a deacon," Jaybone retorted. Lindsey sunk into her seat, deeply ashamed at what had transpired. *Why would he admit he was a deacon acting like that? I can no longer be connected to him,* she thought. Consecration was approaching, and the church went on a twenty-one-day Daniel fast; a religiously rooted, short-term eating plan drawn from the Book of Daniel, in which meat, wine, and other rich foods are avoided in favor of vegetables and water in order to draw the believer closer to God. Lindsey took full advantage of this opportunity. During those three weeks, she fasted, she prayed, and she studied the Word. Towards the end of the fast, Lindsey heard the voice of the Lord speaking to her, saying, *I want you to minister my word to the people.* Lindsey questioned that voice, but she knew what she had heard. She boldly told the Lord, "NO!" *How could she preach the word of God while continuing to blatantly rebel against his will for her?* She wept uncontrollably as something inexplicable came over her.

Jaybone continued working in the streets, and Lindsey continued working at the salon. Though she had no problem securing clientele, the conditions of the salon became an issue. One morning Lindsey arrived at the salon to open up shop only to find that the lights weren't working. She went to the back of the salon and flipped on another switch; still nothing. This normally wouldn't perturb Lindsey; one day without lights would have normally been a small hiccup. But this wasn't the first time. The salon owner, Marie, was having trouble with paying the utilities. Whether it was the result of irresponsibility or legitimate financial troubles, Lindsey didn't know. All she knew was that it was time for her to move on. "I'm just going to close the shop. Sorry, I'll be up there," Marie murmured before hanging up the phone. Lindsey called her co-workers and shared the news. She also embarrassedly called her clients to inform them that they'd have a bad hair day that day. She knew it was only a matter of time before she would put in her notice at Hair It Is salon.

The search for another salon had begun; and in the meantime, Lindsey worked out of her home. Her needs had been simple. She wanted a well-maintained salon in the same area because of the steady flow of traffic. Serendipitously, the building next door from her previous shop was available for rent. She inquired about the building, and the owner agreed to let her rent it. She knew securing the deposit would be a struggle, but she had the support of her husband and a solid clientele that would gladly follow her.

She would do whatever it took to secure the deposit for her salon. Some of her regular clients followed her to her home salon, but it still wasn't enough for the deposit. She needed $3000, and the loss she'd taken from leaving Hair It Is put her in a sticky situation. Her only choice at this point was to go to her husband. It was the least he could do after his countless affairs and abusive behavior. She approached him confidently with a stern look on her face, which edged on being a warning. Inside she was a nervous wreck, though. This conversation could go exceptionally well, or it could be a grave mistake. One never knew with Jaybone.

"If that will put a smile on your face, you'll have it." Jaybone hustled up some of the money plus he had a little help from Willow.

"All she putting you through," Willow said as if he had no part in their dysfunction, "and you going to help her get a shop? You must really love her; I'll give you the $1500." Lindsey's heart dropped when he told her what Willow had said, but she got it together real quick - the girl had slept with her husband after all. She told herself, *if that girl wants to be stupid and give my husband money for me, then I'll let her*. All Lindsey knew is that she wanted that salon open. Willow wasn't the only woman that would give him money, though. "You must believe I'm a fool if you think I only think these girls are giving you money and nothing else." He tried convincing her that he had no other motives; he even devised a plan for he and Lindsey to run a game on the girls. Lindsey reluctantly agreed. They would call a woman, whom he had previously slept with, and tell her that Jaybone was in jail; the woman would then send Lindsey money via MoneyGram and hours later, one of them would pretend that he'd just gotten out. This scheme worked for a moment, but she soon caught on. Growing suspicious, she called the jail to see if he was there. He wasn't. To make matters worse, one day while picking up cash from MoneyGram, Lindsey happened to see a form on the counter with Jaybone's name and address. This wasn't a part of the plan. It turns out Jaybone was running a scheme of his own, syphoning money from another unsuspecting victim. This infuriated Lindsey. She promptly called and cursed him out, only to receive a string of lies in return.

On February 20, 2009, Lindsey became the owner of Royal Favor Hair Salon, Inc. She had the keys in her hands, and the ink had dried on the lease; but she was still uneasy. This was partly because the flow of walk-ins did not measure up to her expectations, but it was also because of the way she had obtained the money for the deposit. *I'm not going to do well here am I God?* She said to herself. Though she knew God would fulfill the desires of her heart, she also knew that if she had truly waited, her desires would not include sorrow or struggle. Lindsey had found herself barely making her lease payments. She did not renew her lease for the next year.

She was on the hunt for another salon. It wasn't too long before she noticed a "for rent" sign in the window of a vacant building. It was an elegant house turned salon on a busy street flooded with other businesses and adjacent to a historic restaurant. The owner was a slender and hospitable man who had purchased the building for his estranged ex to open her own salon. Since they didn't work out, he had no use for the building; so, he gladly turned the keys over to Lindsey. He gave her the option of changing the name or keeping it as is; of course, she had opted for the former. Royal Favor Hair Salon was back in business. She did not pray about this move, but she went with it. It had all come together so smoothly, so to her, it must've been a miracle. She soon had another stylist join her team as well as a nail technician. Business was flourishing, and for the first time in a long time, Lindsey was happy. "With a name like that she must be saved," one client had told her, "so I turned around to see what you were about."

Business was doing well at her shop and Jaybone wanted to buy another car to flip, as they flipped them often. It had been another hustle to add to the repertoire and more income to keep the family afloat. For a moment it seemed as if those dreams that he previously talked about were coming true.

One day Jaybone told Lindsey to call up an old friend from back home to see if he had any cars for sale. "Who dis?" He answered the phone as if the feds were on the other end of the line.

"This Lindsey," she said in a tone that disarmed him.

"Oh, what up doe *baby*?" Lindsey could barely breathe as the blood slid from her lips down to her neck; Jaybone's clenched fist struck her mouth like a rock. With blood gushing down her mouth, she kept talking as if nothing had happened. As if Jaybone had not taken his strong fist and pressed it against her face.

"Oh, I was calling to see if you had any cars for sale; my husband wants to get one." Lindsey mumbled.

"Nope, baby girl. I don't have anything right now, but hit me up later doe." He was cool, amiable, and matter-of-fact, completely oblivious to the fact that his old friend had been struck in the mouth by someone he respected.

"Alright, thanks," she managed to say. "What you hit me for!?" She exclaimed, unable to control her emotions.

Cus, "that nigga called you baby, I know he like you, ya'll trying to play me."

"Jaybone, "I don't like him! You know everybody say that at home." It was true. "What up doe?" was the standard accepted greeting for Detroiters, at least those who resided within the city limits.

"He doesn't like me. You know him and my sister used to kick it." She had a step-sister from her mom's marriage. "I need to go to the hospital; my lip is pretty bad." As much as she wanted to, Lindsey did not retaliate. Her friend Nicole and her daughters were temporarily living with them, and she didn't want them to know what had happened.

"Call me as soon as you're done, and I'll be back to get you." Jaybone didn't even bother to go into the hospital with her. Instead, he left a simple warning: *don't tell anyone what happened*. The nurses were empathetic when they asked her what went on. She made up some lie about falling, and they stitched her up and gave her medication. She called Jaybone to pick her up, and they went back home. She wore a face mask to work, telling her coworkers that she didn't want to spread the germs from her cold. She even faked a cough to make it seem real.

Not too long after her stitches dissolved, her mouth still sore and swollen, Jaybone began kissing her neck and caressing her; begging her to make love to him. If looks could kill, they'd commit the murder she'd sometimes wished on him. She pushed him off, and rolled over and tried drifting off to sleep. He stormed out of the house as if he were the one who'd been assaulted. As if he had been embarrassed. As if he was the one forced to make up lies to hide his crippling shame. Once he was out of the door, Lindsey went over to the mirror and stared at herself. With tears flowing, she shook her head and said, "This is not me." She got back in bed and cried herself to sleep that night, not caring what time it was when he returned. The next morning, she took a picture of herself, and went off to work.

The rain was pouring when Lindsey arrived at the salon, she ducked and dodged while running into the back door, which was where she parked her car. It was the car that Jaybone told Lindsey he bought from a friend, but it turned out to be a car Willow had given him. She had found the title with her name on it hidden under the seat. When she confronted him, sparks flew; and she spat verbal barbs while he filled the air with useless lies.

Once she arrived home from the shop that day, he asked if she had gotten the car washed. "Ummm no," she responded anxiously.

"It looks like somebody washed your car." His temper began to rise.

"I told you, nobody washed my car, it has not moved from the back all day and you know it was raining today," Lindsey said.

"I know what a washed car looks like cus I worked at a car wash before; don't play wit me."

"Well, you must've forgot, cus nobody washed the car." They were both hollering at each other at this point, with him accusing her of messing around with the building owner, Rob.

"No I'm not, and he didn't touch my car," She was crying inconsolably.

"Come on, we going up there." He couldn't be reasoned with. He was a wild bull charging at his own delusions.

Her sister-in-law had been visiting from Florida and petitioned him, "please don't go up to that girl job acting a fool. Think about your family."

"I don't give a f%^* about none of that; somebody washed her car, let's go now!" They drove to the shop, and before Rob could step foot across the threshold, Jaybone irately asked him if he'd washed Lindsey's car. It was more of a statement than a question.

"I don't know what you're talking about man," Rob said.

"Dog, I know what a washed car looks like. I used to work for a carwash, her car been washed."

"I'm sorry, but I haven't been here all day. I just got home from work."

"Yeah you know what, y'all playing games, somebody gonna get hurt. Get yo s!@#; you not working in here no more." Lindsey's heart drop with this unjust command. What would she do without her shop? She had been living her dream, owning Royal Favor Salon; and Jaybone was prepared to strip it from her over an asinine accusation. "Please don't do this. This is my shop where I make my money, why you doing this!?" No pleading could prevent his indignation, though. He had made it up in his mind that the owner wanted more than just rent for the building.

"Y'all tryna play me. Get yo s%^& now I said, I'm not playing." Like a teenager caught defying his parent's rules, Lindsey accepted her punishment and began packing her equipment. She clumsily piled shampoo bottles, curling wands, flat irons, and electric stoves in cardboard boxes. That was the end of salon number two. There she was again, crying herself to sleep. It was becoming a fruitless and exhausting pattern that only left her with more questions than answers. She woke up to her sister-in-law, Macy, who patiently sat on the edge of her bed.

"I'm so sorry you had to go through that. Something is wrong with him," she said. "Is he on drugs?"

"He only smokes weed." Lindsey wiped her sleeve across her tear-stained face, her voice hoarse with the remnants of sleep.

"Naw, he got to be smoking something else acting like that. I know the difference." They sat on the porch for hours talking, with Macy trying and at times succeeding in cheering Lindsey up. Night was approaching, and Jaybone had not returned home. This time Lindsey didn't care.

She was back at her home hair salon; and though she had retained a few customers, it didn't compare to the income she'd been generating by being in an actual salon. She began to get discouraged - both with the economic loss and also with Jaybone's fluctuating devotion to their ministry. They were still going to church, and he was still training to be a deacon; but his lifestyle didn't quite match up to the demands and expectations of a man of God. This filled Lindsey with an unrelenting guilt. Keeping quiet made her an accessory, which left her with no choice but to tell her leaders the truth about her husband.

She told them that he was still running the streets, that he had a secret cell phone, and that he was still messing around with other girls and smoking weed. In other words, she told them that he was not ready to be a deacon. Of course Jaybone was livid; of course he spat venom at his wife, but she didn't care anymore. She even told him she wasn't running the streets anymore, leaving their children in the house while they made out of state runs transporting dope or even worse, taking them on the roads with them. She was serious about her walk with the Lord. "Oh, so you don't care if I take penitentiary chances? You know my license is suspended." Lindsey didn't know whether to laugh or scream at this absurd accusation. She thought to herself, *penitentiary chances? That's petty hustling we've been doing*. She wouldn't dare say this out loud, though. None of this stopped Jaybone's flow. He would take the bus, have his cousin drive him, or he'd even have girls pick him up to make runs. Sometimes, he would take a chance and drive himself. This infuriated Lindsey, who was growing tired of being the good and faithful wife to a man that made it his business to dishonor her. As soon as he arrived at the Chattanooga line to come home to Atlanta, she would get dressed and leave the house. She could be going to the mall or to the movies with a friend or just to the corner store, but she wasn't going to wait around for Jaybone anymore. She was tired of being a doormat - even doormats got more attention than she'd been getting. She didn't even care if no eyes looked her way while on her frivolous adventures, she was just happy to feel like a woman again.

She had been in contact, off and on, with her friend's cousin, Darryl; whom she met at her son's basketball game. He was good-looking with a medium build and average height, not entirely tall, but tall enough for her to be seen with him. He had often inquired about Lindsey, wanting to hook up; but of course she was afraid. If Jaybone had gone ballistic at the *thought* of another man washing her car, what would he do if she had gone on an actual date? Still, he persisted, and eventually, she relented. During one of Jaybone's excursions to Knoxville, Lindsey took him up on his offer; meeting him at a gorgeous hotel outside of Atlanta.

He could smell her tension as they walked passed the grey doors. They were admirably nice-looking and shiny, the numbers glistened as they lay on the brass plates. She wondered what was behind them. *Who else was stepping out on their spouses behind those doors? What other poor man was being cheated on by an unattended wife? Could Jaybone have brought another woman to one of these rooms?* "Lighten up," he said. "It's ok." Her shoulders stood stiff through her white blouse, which was unbuttoned just below her bosom. She had on fitted jeans that hugged her curves to perfection, and she had slicked her hair up into a Nubian bun. She had asked for this, but she still wore a worried look on her face; as if she had been caught in a forest eating the meal of a family of bears.

"Naw, it ain't okay. I don't do stuff like this," she chuckled nervously. He grabbed her and began hugging and kissing her, which left her feeling both pleasured and terrified. She tried to halt the thoughts swimming through her head as he kissed her neck and collarbone. *What would Jaybone do if he caught me? This is wrong. I'm going to hell.* A calculator couldn't add up the number of times Jaybone had stepped outside of their marriage, but here she was drowning in guilt for one indiscretion. "Wait, do you have a condom?" She asked. He pulled them out, and that night she gave herself to another man; falling asleep into his arms like two new lovers.

Dawn had come and she lay there naked under the stiff hotel sheets – just her and Darryl and her guilt. "OH NO! I gotta go!" She exclaimed. She didn't even bother to wake him up before getting dressed and heading home. Once she got there, before checking her messages and tending to her children, she hopped in the shower. Whether it was the water or her tears that washed off that night, she didn't know. All she knew was that the pleasure between her thighs did nothing to heal the pain in her heart. Instead of getting back at Jaybone, she was left right where she started - in pain, devastated, and lonely.

"Your husband been at my house and we just got done making love." Jaybone was away in Knoxville, when Lindsey received the call. One would expect that a woman in that position would be remorseful or embittered or even desperate. She, instead, laughed mockingly and hung up the phone. Lindsey's hands shook as she dialed Jaybone's number. He didn't answer. She kept calling and texting him, stabbing the numbers on the phone with an animalistic fury. When he finally answered, she cursed him out with every foul word she could muster. He went on to tell her that he wasn't with a girl, and that the girl was lying. After all, she did call while he had been away. But it didn't matter to Lindsey. She knew this woman had been sleeping with her husband. Maybe not that day, or even that week, but this girl was her husband's lover.

She packed her and her children's clothes, and that morning they got up and left. She didn't have much money, so she called and asked the bus station if they had a program for domestic abuse situations. The representative at the station told her that he couldn't help her but gave her a number to a place that would. They were able to get a one-way bus ticket to Detroit. She left the car in the Marietta, Georgia Greyhound parking lot with the keys inside. She was done and ready to leave it all behind. When they arrived at her grandmother's house in Detroit, they were weary and disoriented. The ride felt like an eternity with her three children and father who had been visiting in tow. And though she had some brief pangs of believing it was all a mistake, she was happy to be around people who truly loved her. She was happy to be home.

When Jaybone came back from Knoxville, he was met with an empty nest - twigs and leaves and feathers were all that remained. He immediately called Lindsey's phone, but she didn't answer. After several more unanswered calls, he finally had his cousin call her to find out where she had left the car. He had gotten his car back but not his wife. A few days had passed before she would even talk to him. She told him that she wasn't coming back and that she was tired of being hurt, and for the first time, he believed her. She'd made some empty threats before but had never followed through with her plans, and she most definitely hadn't left a car in the middle of nowhere with its keys inside. He pleaded and begged for his family to return. He lamented that he'd never hurt her again. She didn't believe him, but she did indulge him; making demands about the changes he'd need to make. It was a little over a month before Lindsey brought their children back to Atlanta. After bringing them home, she went back to Detroit; both to solidify her resolve, but also to attend the Threshing Floor Conference. The fellowship and fervent prayer was much needed to get through this trajectory in her life. She spent a few more days in Detroit, and eventually decided to go back home.

They were back in the honeymoon phase. Each day was marked with a comforting predictably that underscored any threat of dysfunction. They'd often go on outings to a matinee and dinner afterward, he'd impress her family with his refined sense of humor and childlike joking that her cousins couldn't get enough off. In the midst of these moments, though, he'd have to make a quick run. He was nothing if not dedicated to his family, which never lacked for anything.

One night in a dream, it was revealed that Willow, the girl who had given Jaybone the $1500 and the car, was pregnant with his child. Though it was just a dream, she still confronted Jaybone - the dream had been so vivid and realistic, considering Jaybone's history. "No," had been his answered. But Lindsey did not believe him.

While she was out one day, she happened to open the trunk of their car and saw a pile of pictures. One of them was a photo of Willow in the hospital with a baby - another little boy with Jaybone's face. She never said a word to him about it. She simply kept the picture as proof of his infidelity. She drove three hours to Knoxville – while he was on a run – to confront him and her directly. When she got to Willow's father's house, her brother came to the door and Lindsey asked if she was there. He told her no, and she left. She continued to drive around Knoxville, stopping in their old stomping grounds, desperately searching for her husband. Their old quarters had only been a 12 by 12-inch square, but for Lindsey, the ride felt like an endless maze. After riding around and finding nothing, she received a phone call from Jaybone. 'Why are you in Knoxville going to Willow's daddy's house looking for her, she doesn't even stay there anymore."

"I know she's pregnant by you, so you need to stop lying. I just got to see for myself." Lindsey replied.

"You crazy, you need to go back home."

'You making me crazy, and I ain't crazy, but imma show you crazy. You nasty community d!@# b#$%^!" After the last heady breath of curse words, she hung up the phone. She screamed and cried the entire drive home, her tears and her wails full of anger. She was angry at her husband, but mostly she was angry at herself for still remaining in such a turbulent marriage that not only wounded her but also her children. Her anger rose as her tears fell like lava out of a brimming volcano; and after countless minutes of this man-made disaster, all she felt was numb.

Lindsey's mother Netta was coming to visit, and it was no secret of what was transpiring in their marriage. Lindsey would tell her mother just about everything that was going on between them.

"Does it bother you that Jaybone stays gone for days at a time or stays out all night?"

"We'll momma, it got to the point where I'm glad when he's gone. I don't have to worry about arguing or fighting in front of the children, and it's peaceful in the house. I'm really starting not to care like I used to; sometimes I miss him and sometimes I don't."

"Well Lindsey, like your grandma always said, when you're sick and tired of being sick and tired, you'll do something about your situation. I'm not telling you to leave your husband, but I hate to see ya'll do this in front of my grandchildren…it really hurts me," Netta began to cry. "They don't deserve it."

Lindsey's tears followed Netta's, "I know momma, I know. It won't be long."

It wasn't long before he came home that an argument ensued, seemingly out of nowhere. Their relationship started to be an ugly pattern stitched with dwindling thread. They'd start talking about something inconsequential, which would lead to a topic of contention, a word or phrase mentioned would trigger Lindsey, and Jaybone would retaliate with fits of rage. "What she did to you for you to treat her like this?" Netta intervened hysterically.

He yelled, "That B@#$! Gonna pay till the day she dies!"

"JAYBONE!" Netta said.

With tears in her eyes, Lindsey reminded him of that one thing. That one thing that filled him with uncontrollable bitterness. "I done paid enough for what you still holding on to way back in 1992."

In 1992, Lindsey was introduced to Brent, a dangerously tall, dark, and handsome, hazel-eyed boy whom she met through her distant cousin, Shar. It was another Detroit summer, humid, sunny, and lively - the perfect setting for mischief of the romantic variety. Lindsey was dating Jaybone, and Shar had a boyfriend; but they were young and in relationships that oscillated between irreverent uncertainty and stout security. Because Lindsey and Jaybone had a son, theirs was a bit sticky, but they still had their share of problems. As it turns out, Jaybone had cheated on her with Shar's friend while Shar cheated on her boyfriend with Jaybone's friend, Lo, only adding to the twisted web of summer infidelity. Lindsey found this to be the perfect opportunity to have some fun of her own, so she slept with Brent. It was her only sexual experience outside of her two long-term relationships. She ended up being swallowed in their wanton passion. The revenge she'd pursued only made matters worse. Jaybone was so distraught after she told him, that he moved away temporarily. Though they got back together, he'd never let her live it down. It was simply more brush for his uncontrollable fire.

After that commotion, Jaybone stormed out of the house. That next day, Lindsey told her mother that she was getting a divorce. "Are you sure that's what you want to do?"

"Ma, the baby is his."

"Aww naw, Lindsey. For real? "How do you know?"

"I spoke to the girl's foster mother and she sent me a picture of the baby, and it looks just like Jaybone. I wrote him a long letter, but the Lord said wait before I give it to him."

"I do believe if you let him know all this right now, he will kill you!"

Lindsey said, "Yeah I feel the same way. That's why the Lord said wait." So, she remained silent. She hadn't told her mother about the possibility that Jaybone was also the father to Willow's child. That would have broken her.

To deliver on her proclamation of divorce, she made a plan. She began looking for apartments and stealthily put away her belongings. She still, however, acted as his wife. She still cooked dinner, she still made plates, she still washed clothes, was pleasant in her conversation, and she still made love to him. The pressures of pretending started to take a toll on her though. One day while driving on the freeway, she had to pull the car over because her heart was aching badly. In the days leading up to this, her heart would feel as if it were in knots and she often felt as if she was going to pass out. They were only panic attacks, but she woke up many days wishing they were more. One day after waking up alive she pleaded, *Lord, why do you let me live? I just want to die…just let me die…!*

After waiting over a month in silence, the day came for her to give him the letter. It was one week after his birthday, so he was nicer than usual. His "letter of resignation" was about 200 hundred words but had one ardent message, *it was time to vacate the premise*s. He went ballistic, calling her every foul name that he could muster. After gathering his belongings, he grabbed a machete and started swinging it in the air. After a few warning swings, he went straight for the leather furniture slitting the couch, the loveseat and a few chairs to their dining room table. He then threw a tool that hit Lindsey in the leg, leaving her with a bloody gash. Their children stepped into the chaos with desperation and furious innocence. They shed their own tears while Jada tried consoling her mother. Jaybone remained irate. Blind to the chaos he'd just caused, he picked up his stuff, got in his car, and sped off.

The next day, Lindsey got an order of protection and sent out a mass text petitioning her friends and family to fast and pray with her as she went through a divorce. She often sent out these frantic texts, so she knew there was a chance that her folks would think it was another false alarm. She informed her leaders and a few other church members about her decision, and all communication was cut off between Jaybone and her. She still allowed her children to talk to him – if only to avoid their resenting her by keeping them from their father.

The holidays were approaching and of course the children wanted daddy home. It started with, "my dad wants to know if you are doing okay." "My dad wants to know if he can pick us up and take us to the movies." "My dad wants to know…" After a few innocent visits to appease the kids, it then became, "mom can my dad spend the night in our room pleeease? He said he won't bother you." Maybe it was because of the sheer joy on Jada's face or the way her teeth gleamed when she held her e's a little too long, but whatever it was, Lindsey agreed. She let him spend one night in bed with her children, and as promised, he didn't bother her. That one night turned into many other nights, and eventually, he found his way back in their bedroom. She had the order of protection dropped and didn't proceed with the divorce. He was enrolled in anger management classes, which he was close to finishing, and Lindsey signed up too as a show of solidarity. She mostly just listened to other women's stories in these classes as she wasn't going for herself anyway, but for him.

He had this manipulating and persuasive appeal about himself that made women do just about anything he wanted. Everything was going great, but Lindsey knew it wouldn't last long.

"We just don't know what this is." The doctor looked puzzled as he shared Lindsey's "normal" test results. She had been dealing with severe abdominal pains for months. They sometimes felt worse than her labor pains. Exactly the first three days of every month, it was as if she were having contractions, which was followed by vomiting. Pain medications didn't make a dent. She would lay in a fetal position, rocking, moaning, and crying until she fell asleep. She finally broke down and asked Jaybone for some marijuana; the numbing effect made her pain somewhat bearable.

Because her appointments were scheduled right before or after the pain came, it was hard for the doctors to determine anything conclusive. After weeks of pain and unanswered prayers, Lindsey concluded that she was being punished by God for going back to the hell that he'd deliver her from. One of the doctors even asked if she was pregnant, which she wasn't. But even though she wasn't physically pregnant, she believed that she was birthing something spiritual because it seemed like the attacks in her marriage were becoming worse. She would always be on the search for something; some clue that would lead her towards his mischief. And as she went looking, she found it. She searched through cell phones, wallets, cars, and clothes, and when she discovered her evidence, she confronted him with it. Whether she cursed him out or straight hit him, they often started fighting after these encounters. Sometimes these arguments went no further than yelling contests, other times they were horrific. During one argument provoked by his infidelity, Jaybone got so angry that he took a shot at her in their bedroom; the bullet barely missed her head as it shot through the wall. Their church leaders begged him to hand the gun over, but he never did.

It was tax time, and Lindsey had both filed and received her return. She didn't want to tell Jaybone the total amount because she didn't want to invest in his drug schemes anymore. She wanted to do the right thing this time. She had an instinct, or perhaps it was God, telling her to send a copy of her return to her mom's house, so he wouldn't find it. Lindsey ignored that voice and instead switched hiding places around their house, desperate to find the most inconspicuous location. She needed to make a grocery run before her upcoming doctor's appointment, so she quickly hid the papers along with her gun in their boys' room in the far back corner of their bunk bed.

"So, do you have something to tell me?" Jaybone roared. He sounded angsty and intimidating, and she knew there was only one reason why.

"What are you talking about?" She asked with faux surprise.

"Don't play dumb with me, you know what the f*&# I'm talking about! You been playing me, huh? Yeah okay, I'll just wait for you to get back home." She was a nervous wreck, especially since he had her gun. She fidgeted her way back to their driveway and went upstairs to their bedroom, hopefully able to diffuse the situation. With the tax return papers in his hand, he asked, "So what did you do with the rest of the money?"

"I paid bills and bought y'all stuff."

"You lying, yo' trick b!@#$ a%$ probably gave it to some nigga."

"I don't have no nigga to give it to," her voice cracked and the waterworks began. Slow, singular tears danced down her face.

"I'm bout to call the pastor and see what he got to say about your fake Christian a#%."

"Hello," Pastor Jones answered.

"Pastor Jones, you know Lindsey is supposed to be a Christian, and she lied to me about her income tax money."

"Well let's calm down first Brother Wise." There was no use, because as soon as Jaybone uncovered a stale moment, he unleashed a fury of insults and cries of betrayal and an arrogant indignation only typical of despots. Still, Pastor Jones remained resolute. "Did you ask

Sister Wise what she did with the money she didn't tell you about and why she lied?"

"She said she paid the bills and bought us stuff, but she didn't say why she lied to me. Imma kill this girl for playing with me, and I'm out here taking chances for my family." His rage became more pronounced with each syllable, making it hard to tell if he was just being dramatic or if he truly felt betrayed.

"Let me talk to Sis Wise." He passed Lindsey the phone. "Hello, Sis Wise."

"Yes," she said, surprisingly unbothered.

"Now I heard what Brother Wise had to say, so why didn't you tell him how much money you really got back?" Though annoyed that this gross display of his disrespect had become a counseling session, she still obliged.

"Well, I didn't tell him because I didn't want him to flip my money anymore."

"So, what did you do with the money you didn't tell him about?"

"I paid bills off, bought him three suits, the kids some clothes, and myself one suit."

"Ok. That sounds like the right thing to do with the money." Their exchange had been as matter-of-fact as parents trying to get to the bottom of some injustice brought on by their young children. Jaybone, sensing this assault to his ego, became livid again.

"*That sound good*? Nigga she lied to me and you just told me that I had a right to be mad now you telling her that's good! So, you wanna be on her side now..."

"That's not what I..."

"Instead of telling her she was wrong."

Pastor Jones remained cool, assured, and only focused on the facts. "She was wrong for not being truthful with you, but what she did with the money, I do believe was ok."

"Yeah y'all must be f!@#$*%. It's cool, I got something for you and her b#$@! a#%! Ya'll wanna play games wit me? Nigga I'm from Detroit! I'm on my way to your house."

"Brother Wise, I'm asking you not to come to my house acting like that."

"Well how about I come to the church and take care of all y'all fake a@# Christians." His panting and pacing turned into something more horrifying "But I got something for Lindsey now. Ya'll wanna hear this?" CLACK! CLACK! He cocked his gun back.

"Give me my gun Jaybone!" Lindsey exclaimed.

"I ain't giving you s*&#," he said.

"I gotta go to my doctor's appointment. I can't miss it," Lindsey cried. He let her leave, and she did not return. After hours of her being gone, he called her several times. Instead of returning his calls, she dialed the police and told them that her husband had her gun and was in the house with their kids and that she was afraid to go home because he might kill her. They advised her not to go back to the house until they had him apprehended. Within 30 minutes, their house was surrounded by Atlanta's SWAT team, helicopters, and the Local News. Her life was now an episode of *COPS*. Jaybone managed to get out of the house without the police noticing. When she turned on the news that night, the moniker:

"Estranged husband takes wife's gun in domestic dispute"

along with his picture, dashed across the screen. She went from being disturbed to completely humiliated, receiving a flood of calls from concerned family and friends. Lindsey didn't feel safe staying in the house that night, so her and her children stayed at a hotel. The police advised her to tell Jaybone to turn himself in in order to prevent a tragedy. When they got settled, she discovered that under the bed was the worst hiding spot; it had been Jaybone's hiding spot too.

The next day she learned that Jaybone had turned himself in. She had also gotten word that he returned to Knoxville after being released from jail, so she was forced to move out of their house and into an apartment. It would be her first place to herself. She was starting a life without her high school sweetheart, the father of her children, the one to whom she said "I Do." The apartment was a simple two bedroom flat in a quiet part of the city.

The boys were cozy in one room and Jada and she were in another, but still the place felt large and hollow inside. Though she was left with no choice, she began to miss having access to her husband; believing that she couldn't make it alone. She would stay in bed, cry, and sleep most of the day while her children were off at school. Their marriage was a tumultuous one, but it was all she knew. Still, she made peace with her choice as she knew their hell of a union was not ordained by God.

It was the beginning of the month, and her pains had returned after weeks of believing she was in the clear. "Momma, do you want me to take you to the doctor? I don't have to go to school." Malik said during their drive to school; she had been crying nonstop.

"No son, I'll drive myself; you need to be at school, but somebody is going to tell me what's going on because I can't take this pain any longer." After dropping him off, she headed to her gynecologist's office. She didn't have an appointment, but the pain had become so unbearable that she was willing to take the risk. Of all the days, they were closed that day, but there was another gynecologist office in the same plaza; so, she went in as a walk-in patient. It has been said that some of the best hair stylists have the most unkempt hair because they devote the whole of their energy to serving their clients instead. Lindsey wished this was her excuse. Her hair was frazzled, her eyes were puffy, black rings replaced the thin skin under her eyes, and her skin was pale. She hadn't even bothered to consider her attire. She wore a worn, grey sweatshirt and green jogging pants with old sneakers. If one didn't know any better, they'd have mistaken her for a drug addict. She approached the front desk of the office, kneeling down and in tears. "Sorry I don't have an appointment, but I'm in excruciating pain. Can I please see a doctor? I will wait."

She expected side eyes from onlookers in the waiting area, but instead she received empathetic cries of, "let her go, let her go." The receptionist took her information and told her that someone would be with her shortly. She crawled on the floor to a chair and kneeled over the seat, rocking back and forth. They called her to the back, and the doctor begin asking her questions, which she answered through grunts and sighs. He asked her if she wanted pain medication, but she'd already been down that road to no avail.

"Have you tried birth control pills?"

"Yes, I have, and it doesn't help. All my tests came back normal."

"Okay, I'm going to order a vaginal ultrasound, and I'll see you back in two weeks. I think I know what this is."

"Okay, thank you for taking me like this."

She returned to the office two weeks later as directed. "Hello, I'm Dr. George nice to meet you Mrs. Wise."

"Hello," she said puzzledly, but you met me two weeks ago."

"OH MY GOD! That was you in the lobby on the floor?"

"Yes sir."

"Well you were really hurting!"

"Yes, I was."

"I would have never known that was you, you don't even look like the same lady. Let's get you taken care of." He performed more tests and took more samples. When he returned, a reassuring expression adorned his face.

" From my findings, you have what is called Adenomyosis."

"WHAT?" In her mind she translated it as something that meant she only had one month to live.

"Well," he chuckled, "unlike Endometriosis, which is a disorder in which the tissues that normally line the uterus grow outside of the uterus, Adenomyosis is tissue that exists within and grows into the uterine wall." Lindsey took a sigh of relief. She knew what endometriosis was, she had known other women with this condition. "Here are your options. First, how many children do you have?"

"Three," she said.

"Do you planning on having any more?"

"No."

"Are you sure?"

"I'm positive."

"Well a hysterectomy will cure the problem, or you can take birth control and treat it with pain medication: it's your choice." Lindsey took in the somewhat musty air of the office room. She'd known the pain had to be part of a bigger problem, but she wasn't expecting surgery. "But the way I saw you in here two weeks ago, I'm pretty sure this is very painful," he said.

"Yes, it is."

"Well, take some time to think it over and call my office to let me know what you decide."

"I don't need to think it over, I want to have the hysterectomy."

"Are you positive Mrs. Wise, because there is no reversal for this, you understand that?" His face grew serious, and he gave her a look that made her feel as if she were being sentenced for some petty crime.

"Yes sir, I'm ready to get over this pain."

"Okay, your ovaries are good, so I'll just remove your uterus and leave your ovaries, we'll do a partial hysterectomy." Lindsey brimmed with relief. She was a woman who was about to undergo an invasive surgery, yet she felt as if it were one of the best days of her life. "Once we get a clearance from your insurance, we will call you for a date to come in for pre- op testing and a surgery date. Take care."

"Thank you, Dr. George."

It was October and Jaybone's birthday was approaching. The children had begged and pleaded to see their father on his birthday, so Lindsey gave in and told them yes. She went all out, cooking his favorite meal:

shrimp, crab legs, and a lobster tail, all while thinking, *why am I doing this to myself?* She had even bought him a birthday cake. They sat at the table and had dinner as a family, which felt strange to Lindsey. She hadn't expected butterflies, but she also didn't expect to feel so removed from him; he'd only been gone for a few months. After dinner, he slept in the room with the boys instead of making the three-hour drive back to Knoxville. Lindsey didn't mind because he'd been a gentleman the entire night.

The next morning when Lindsey returned from taking the kids to school, Jaybone and she found themselves together in her bed. She made sure they had protection. He fell asleep, and she showed no signs of following suit, so she sat up reading. As she sat with her back against the headboard, and her leg dangling over the bed, her foot brushed over his unopened bag. She peered down at it, convincing herself that because it wasn't closed, she technically wouldn't be invading his privacy; so, she unzipped the bag and looked through it. Beneath his jeans, a toothbrush, and a t-shirt, was a birthday card from Willow that read, "we love you daddy" as well as a sex toy. *We.* She didn't say anything to him, but she put the stuff back in a way that showed she'd seen it.

She woke up to an irate Jaybone, the Jaybone she'd known and endured for over a decade. He cursed her out, threatened her, took her phone, and pushed the birthday cake off of their table before grabbing his bag. "Why did you go through my f@#$&*% bag?"

"Get out of my house cus you ain't gone neva change!" Lindsey exclaimed. She managed to get her phone and push him out the door, locking it at record speed. BOOM! He kicked the door in, almost knocking it off of its hinges. He wore a sinister expression on his face, celebrating her humiliation.

"Na b!@#$, that's what the f@#$ you get for going through my s*&#."

She was back to where she'd started. "I'm calling the police!" She hollered as she dialed both the apartment's office and the police. He eventually left, and the apartment maintenance repaired the door. She had to file another restraining order for that property.

Lindsey sat her children down and talked with them about everything that had happened. They were shaken up and broken-hearted. After a few silent moments, she looked up at them, "Y'all know men are not supposed to mistreat women like that."

"Yes momma," the boys said.

"How do ya'll feel when your dad says and does mean things to me?"

Her oldest son Malik seethed, "It makes me mad; I want to beat him up."

Her youngest son Jordan said, "I be sad."

Her daughter Jada said, "I be sad too mommy."

"Why don't you leave him momma?" Malik said, teary-eyed.

"Cause I don't have enough strength, and because I still love him." Her chest constricted as she uttered the words, ashamed for meaning them. She had known the man since high school. They shared three children. Their families were intertwined. She hugged her children, told them that she loved them, gave them kisses, and said goodnight. After waking up the next morning, the first thing she prayed was, "Lord, you're going to have to help me get through this." When she went to the bathroom to get ready for the day, she found her feet soaked in a pool of water. She went to the boy's bathroom, and it was full of water too; ants were coming out the sockets of both bathrooms, and ants were everywhere in the kitchen. She called the apartment office to inform them of the issue. They sent maintenance over with Shop Vacs and blowers. They also sprayed the apartment to get rid of the ants. Her and her children lived like that for days. Mold had formed in the boy's bathroom from the water damage, and despite attempts to annihilate them, the ants weren't going away. When she called the apartment office again, she learned that they had never experienced a problem like that in any of their properties. It was a nice, gated apartment complex in a quiet suburb. Still, Lindsey refused to pay rent until they solved her problem. They offered to move them into another building in the complex instead of her breaking the lease. She didn't take the offer. In some way, Lindsey felt that she was being punished for letting Jaybone back in when she'd been praying to be released from his indomitable grip.

The apartment manager informed Lindsey that he would take her to court if she didn't pay the rent. Lindsey took pictures and had dates of everything that happened. She had kept the receipts for the rent she paid plus her deposit. She ended up winning the case over the apartment complex. *God, still loves me*, she whispered to herself. They refunded all of her money, plus the judge awarded her pain and suffering, and breaking the lease was not reported on her credit report. Still, she had to move out and didn't know where they were going to live. Netta really wanted them to move back to Knoxville, but Lindsey refused. To her Knoxville had been a battleground, loamy soil filled with skulls and bones that she had no intention of revisiting. She told her mom, "you know I hate Knoxville cause' if I see any of those girls, we gonna be fighting."

Her mother reassured her, "Girl, don't you know that God will fix it so you could be in the same place with one of those girls and never run into them?" Her wisdom was that of another God-fearing woman who had suffered from unspeakable abuse.

"Yeah, I know that, but I just don't like Knoxville."

"Lindsey, you know ya'll don't have to be living like that."

"I know momma, we'll be alright." One of her church members, Sis Tee, offered for them to move in with her and her nephew. It would be five people living in a two-bedroom apartment. She had no other options, though, so she put her belongings in storage and moved in with Sis Tee. She moved the boys' bunk bed in, and Jordan slept on the top bunk while Jada and Lindsey shared the bottom. Malik slept on the couch in their bedroom, or sometimes he slept on the air mattress in the living room. At this point, it didn't matter to Lindsey. Even in a crowded home, they were happy, they were safe, and they were free.

Time passed, and Lindsey received a call from Dr. George's office with her surgery date. On October 29, 2009, Lindsey had a partial hysterectomy. She was sore and a bit sedated when she woke up from the surgery, and she could no longer have children, but she was no longer in pain. Somehow Jaybone caught wind that his wife was in the hospital having her reproductive organs removed, so he showed up for support. She stayed in the hospital for three days, and once she was released and back to her cramped new living space, the two of them sat on the couch and talked. In the middle of their conversation, the doorbell rang. It was Lady Jones. The look on her face was as if she'd seen a ghost. She didn't know that Lindsey had told Jaybone where they were living.

"Hi Brother Wise," she said.

"Hi Mother Jones."

"How you feeling Lin?" she asked.

"I'm feeling ok. Just a little sore."

"Well I'm not going to stay long. I just came to check on you."

"Ok, thank you," Lindsey said. The look Lady Jones gave her told Lindsey that they'd be having a talk later. That night, there were six people crowded in a two-bedroom apartment. Jaybone stayed over holding Lindsey the entire night. The next morning, he left quietly.

Later that day, Lady Jones did have a talk with Lindsey. She explained to her that she and Pastor Jones were concerned for her safety and that they didn't want to see anything happen to her or the children. Lindsey said, "I know, I know he just came down for the surgery and nothing else. I promise. I pray that the Lord will kill him anyway."

"Is he dead yet?"

"No."

"Well quit praying that prayer, because the Lord is not hearing you. He will take care of Bro Wise in His own way."

"So, Mother Jones, I can't have any friends?"

"You don't need any friends, you need to take this separation time to focus on God, yourself, and your children."

"Well, what if I meet someone, I gotta test him out first?"

"You don't need to test anything out, God knows exactly what you need - even in the sex area. Just focus on you Lin, I love you girl."

"I love you too."

Lindsey's church had recently gone on a Daniel fast, which served as an impetus for her to focus on herself and her health: mentally, physically, spiritually, and emotionally. She began a daily exercise regimen Monday through Friday and sometimes on Saturdays. She walked for an hour, having a conversation with the Lord, clearing her mind, and just enjoying nature. Afterwards, she would go to the apartment exercise room and work on the machines. This not only helped to heal her body, but it also helped to relieve the boulder-like stress from the separation. She talked to the Lord just like she talked with her friends, straightforward and real, withholding nothing. On one walk while talking to the Lord, she asked if it was his will for her to remarry, and of course she told Him who she wanted this man to be. He had to be faithful, hardworking, saved and God-fearing, sexually adept, accepting of her children, always honest, never abusive, not jealous, not controlling - she wanted the perfect man. She heard the Lord say, "there is no perfect man of this nature, but there is a man that will be perfect for you." She smiled and chuckled at herself. She knew this was a list of perfection. Of course, abuse would not be tolerated in her next relationship, but she knew it wouldn't be all flowery meadows either. "I hear you Lord," she responded as she finished her walk. One Saturday, Lindsey and a few other church members went to the underground Atlanta, an underground shopping district that is part tourist trap and part weekend hotspot for AT-aliens looking for a good time. One of the member's son, Rob, was in town and joined them. He inquired about Lindsey, and they engaged in small talk with a bit of flirting in between. Later that night, they all went to a neighborhood bar and grill. He and Lindsey talked the whole time and exchanged numbers before they left. Soon they were having regular phone conversations as he lived in Chicago. He started to fall for Lindsey, and she relished the attention. He was a charming gentleman with a good job working for the White Sox, and he kept her mind off of Jaybone; but she knew he'd only be in her life for a season. Their romance faded quietly. He'd make some woman insanely happy one day, but that woman wasn't Lindsey.

The church was on another 21-day Daniel fast, and she continued her same routine of exercising, fasting, praying and receiving revelations. This time though, she didn't petition Him about her love life, she just fell to her knees and said, "whatever you want me to do Lord, I will do it." She asked the Lord to completely take cursing out of her mouth because she was showing her children that it was okay to curse and praise the Lord using the same tongue. If she wanted them to follow her as she followed Christ, then she'd have to set the right example. Day by day, she found herself free from using profane language. It seemed like overnight her vocabulary had changed. She also found herself waking up in the midnight hours reading His word and writing down whatever the Spirit gave her. It got so heavy that she said, "Okay, you gonna have to stop waking me up like this, I gotta get up and get us ready for school and work." She'd forgotten that she said she'd do whatever the Lord wanted her to do. He continued to visit her, with dreams, with visions, and with His voice. In one vision, He showed her the blessings that He had for her in

His hand but that they'd only be released to her when she followed His plan. Lindsey took this to mean that they should stay in Atlanta because she felt that the Lord was opening doors when He allowed her to get into another salon.

One day while returning home from dropping the kids at school, she saw a large and luxurious salon for rent. She called the owner and they met at the location. The owner immediately took a liking to Lindsey and told her that she wanted to get someone in the shop soon because she was losing money from it being unoccupied. Lindsey was honest and upfront about only having a one-person set-up. The owner told her it was no problem, that she'd buy her whatever she needed to get the business running. Lindsey's heart overflowed with both gratitude and awe. Months before, her sister-in-law had called and told her to meet her because she was paying for her to go have lunch.

"Just you and the Lord," she said. "Just listen to what He has to say to you." She told her to get a binder with her future salon's name on it and everything that she wanted in her salon because she would one day meet someone that would give her all that she desired. When Tisha first told her this, her eyes welled – she'd already had the binder, including the pictures of how her future salon would look! This was nothing but prophetic in her eyes. Her sister-in-law also told her that she saw her with a man – not her brother – and they were living in a big house with the proverbial white fence surrounding it. Lindsey felt obliged to heed to her sister-in-law's predictions. In the past, her prophecies concerning her brother had manifested with a pointed accuracy. This, among other things, made Lindsey grateful that she had great relationships with Jaybone's family, even if they had been separated. From her sister's prophecy, along with the shop owner's attitude and generosity toward her, she took it as a sign that this was where she was destined to be. Still, she had one more thing to do.

Soon after she received the offer, Lindsey spoke with her church leaders about it, and they came up to the building to pray with her. Lindsey had been stuck on the fact that her and her children were living in a cramped apartment. She'd be paying rent for a salon though she didn't even have her own house. After speaking with her leaders, Lindsey accepted the offer – she was back in a salon. She hired another stylist and looked to hire more. They had a steady flow of clients, and the place was getting closer and closer to being the salon that she'd envision. Everything was going as planned, and Lindsey was determined not to move back to Knoxville. To save money for a new apartment, she accepted a part-time job at Wal-Mart while picking up supplies for the salon. It didn't take long for her to secure the deposit for her apartment, and soon after, she had the money to pay the balance. She was all ready to move in when she clearly heard the voice of the Lord say, "MOVE!" Lindsey had heard God's voice in her soul from as long as she could remember, and she rarely ignored it. This time though, His voice was a thunder – it was unambiguous and profound. She knew that she'd have to listen. Her eyes painted with tears, she called her leaders and told them what the Lord had told her. "Well Lin, we don't want to see you go, but we can't argue with the Lord," they said. "We love y'all, but you got to do what the Lord is telling you to do." Lindsey sat silently, convincing her mind that it wasn't His voice at all. That somehow, she'd misheard. Somehow, she was mistaken. She vowed to herself that she would never move back to Knoxville again. "Now, because you are moving," they continued, "don't mean you won't ever come back here, but you have to be obedient, and we can't get in trouble because we want you to stay. Ya'll gonna be alright." With that, Lindsey called her mother and asked if the offer was still open for them to move in. Of course it was. Lindsey also asked if she could bring the children up first while she finished her two weeks at Wal-Mart.

"Now you know you can," Netta said.

Lindsey put in a two weeks' notice at Wal-Mart, she put her remaining furniture in storage, and she sold the salon furniture. They packed their car up, and off they went to the place that she swore she'd never return. As it turns out, the owner of the salon building had been diagnosed with cancer and was getting rid of the building.

Though she was happy to see her mom when she arrived, she wasn't happy to be in Knoxville. She couldn't fake her disappointment as she looked around and saw that everything was the same. The rolling hills with quaint homes atop them, the narrow streets, the sporadic restaurants, the faint silhouette of the Smoky Mountains betrayed her reality. Hers had been a medium-sized apartment with battle marks and war wounds. Hers was only a few friends and some real enemies. Her mother's home was the only saving grace. It was a three-bedroom haven on a steep hill. The smell of the place was a mixture of the expensive cigars her father-in-law chain smoked and the inviting aroma of her mother's homemade meals. It was lined with seasonal candles and beautiful furniture. Each room had a theme and awaited guests. While at her mom's house over the weekend – she'd still been finishing out her work at Wal-Mart throughout the week – she received a phone call from a credit card merchant company trying to sell her a machine for the salon. "Hello, is this Royal Favor Hair Salon?"

"Yes this is."

"May I speak to the owner?"

"Speaking."

"This is Michael from Credit Authorization Services. Is your company set up to receive credit card transactions?"

"Yes sir, we are." He asked what her rates were and began to give her the rates his company was offering.

"Now that I've went over the business portion of this call, may I ask you a question off the record?"

"Sure," she said.

"Are you saved because with a name like Royal Favor, I said to myself, 'she has to be a believer.'" He had a pleasant hoarseness to his voice, an ease when he spoke.

She chuckled and said, "Yes, I am."

"I knew it."

"Well this call wasn't by chance, I'm also a pastor in Charlotte, NC. How many children do you have?"

"Three." Though intrigued, Lindsey was a bit dubious.

"You had a rough pregnancy with your daughter," he stated. She hadn't told him the sex of her children. "But it wasn't a mistake that she was born," he continued. With this statement, she didn't know whether to be disturbed or relieved. "She was destined to be here, and she will be great. Do you have a daughter?" He then asked.

"Uh, yes sir," tears rolled down her face.

"You will not have to worry about her, that pregnancy was not in vain. I also see you contemplating a move?"

"Yes," she said through sobs.

"God said it is time for you to move."

"I'm in the process of moving now, but I was trying to move to Charlotte, I've submitted resumes to various hospitals already."

"I don't see that is where the Lord wants you to be, I see you moving somewhere else. You need to trust God's plan in this move." Lindsey began nodding her head as if this mystery man were sitting right across from her. As if they weren't strangers at all. *How could a stranger know this much about me?*

"May I pray with you?"

"Yes sir," she said. After the prayer, he told Lindsey to take down his personal number and keep in touch with him on her progress. "Thank you sir." They ended the call. Lindsey often prayed to God to give her sign after sign letting her know if what she'd been doing was right. After that phone call, she felt assurance that she was making the right move.

Lindsey made it back to Georgia and went to file for a divorce. She didn't have money for a lawyer, so she researched how to file for a divorce inexpensively. Per her research, she went downtown and filed for divorce by publication; the divorce would be announced in the paper and Jaybone would have 30 days to respond and contest it, or she could move forward without him. He wasn't much of a reader, so she had a good chance of moving forward with the divorce. She went before the judge to explain why she deserved the divorce and also attended a class about children, family, and divorce. This time she didn't tell a soul. She didn't send out any mass texts to her family and friends, asking them to pray and fast with her. She didn't even talk to her pastors. The Lord told her to be silent, that this was between Him and her. As bad as she wanted to tell her mom and best friends, she couldn't. She felt at times she needed their encouragement, but God reminded her to be faithful. This test would be an independent one; *this was not an open book group test.* December 18, 2009, was her last day living in Georgia.

PART III: The Permissive Will

Chapter Seven: Follow The Instructions

It was Christmas in Knoxville, about 40 degrees and not a trace of snow. Still, one could not escape the pageantry of beaming lights or the festive hodgepodge of evergreens, ceramic soldiers, glass bulbs, and Santa Clauses that adorned the streets of nearby Pigeon Forge. Christmas had surely arrived outside, but inside the Wise home, it was more bah humbug. Money was short, and Lindsey was unable to provide the lavish Christmases she once had. This was painful for her, but her children still showed gratitude, thankful for whatever knick knacks they received. The holiday passed uneventfully, and the New Year had arrived. She got her children enrolled in school, and she began her job search. Every day she woke up at 5am to pray, she went to the gym to work out, she took the kids to school, and went to the library and career center seeking employment. She was determined to move out of her mom's house within one year. Jaybone caught wind of their arrival, and he and Lindsey resumed communication. He told her that she was a good wife and mother and that he was sorry for everything he had done to her. "I think you were the strong one, because I don't know if I could've taken all the stuff you took."

This was the first thing he'd been right about in the decade plus of their anarchy disguised as a marriage. Though her instinct was to curse him, to amputate his ego and reciprocate the hell that he had taken her through, she breathed instead, and said something that would shock even the most devout Christians. "Please forgive me for anything that I've ever done to hurt you." At that point they made a silent pact. They would never have that same love relationship again, but they understood that in this life, they were together. They shared children, and they had shared a life, no matter how rocky.

Jaybone would sometimes get the children on the weekends and spend time with them at a nearby hotel. Those visits went from seeing the children to him and Lindsey seeing each other every now and then, as Lindsey would sneak to see him at the hotel while the children were in school. Soon, their platonic understanding turned into a clandestine love affair. Though she knew it was wrong, she justified it by telling herself that she was technically still married and had no desire to meet anyone anytime soon, thus committing adultery again. Still, she knew this was her stronghold, the only thing keeping her from being completely free of him. She added to her daily prayer for the Lord to remove all her sexual desires for Jaybone, and she stopped meeting him as much.

One day, Netta, her cousin Barbie, and she were standing outside of Lindsey's house when two girls came up to them and asked Barbie if she could marry them. She gave a strange look at them and said, "Naw, I don't do that."

The girls then went to Netta and asked her if she could marry them. Netta said, "We don't do that."

One of the girls walked over to Lindsey and said, "You are white."

Lindsey looked at the girl and said, "No I'm not white, I'm black."

The girl then said, "Yes you are, you know that white girl, you need to forgive her." Lindsey woke up in a cold sweat. She had been dreaming.

While at the library one day, she received a phone call from Jaybone. He asked her if she would call this girl for him and ask her a few questions. That girl was Lilith, the white girl from her dream, and the first girl whose house Lindsey charged into. Lindsey called the number and she answered the phone. "Oh my God, Lilith?!" Lindsey exclaimed.

"Is this Lindsey?"

"I don't know why Jaybone told me to call you."

Lilith said, "me either, so don't call my phone no more, you had your chance with Jaybone, and you couldn't be by his side like this white girl could, so that's your problem." Lindsey's face went numb as she hung up the phone. She had called with a positive disposition, perhaps even clearing the air. She was in a different space now. Lilith called back only to reach Lindsey's voicemail but chose to leave a message instead:

Don't be getting smart with Jaybone messing with white girls cause this white girl loves him more than you ever have. S@#! just f@!%#& up right now cause he's married to your mean a$#. I can't be with him while he's married to you cause it's wrong. But don't get it twisted I love him with all my heart and always have...he is a good person but you could never bring that out of him and he tries to have a good heart and do right.

Lindsey called her back and she got her voicemail. "Lilith, I don't know how you would feel if you were married and always catching your husband cheating on you. I don't know if you would sit back and not react to the things you saw and heard, so if you wanna call me a mean a#$, then I'll be one; but until you have a husband, you won't have a clue what I went through." Lindsey's voice was solid, clear, and sure. "I just want you to know that I forgave you for whatever was done while Jaybone and I were together, but if that's what you want, you can have him because I'm done." She ended it with, "I'll keep you in my prayers," and hung up the phone.

Hours later, she got a call back from a hysterical Lilith. "I am so sorry, Jaybone is crazy! He came over to my uncle's house cursing and threatening them, and my uncle called the police on him. I really want to leave him alone, but I'm afraid." Lindsey sat empathetically, listening to Lilith. "I want to get myself right with God. He beat me up bad one time and put me up in a hotel for a week because I was afraid to show my face." Lindsey continued to listen through cathartic sobs, but somehow the phone got disconnected. She called back only to reach Lindsey's voicemail again, so she left another text message:

I apologize for all of this drama. I respect what you said and wont b callin ur phone or txtn you. Thank you for your prayers and please continue to pray for me

and my family and im not bein smart Lindsey we really need it. Im trying to change my life and have been for a long time. i wish the best for u and yours and I hope you have a good evening. please pray for me.

Lindsey texted Lilith back and told her that she'd be praying for her, and their conversation ended. Lindsey was in the parking lot of the library and she threw her hands up and began to cry out to God in thanks as she could actually feel the burden being lifted off of her shoulders. From that day forward, Lindsey sent Lilith Bible verses and encouraging words. She must have told Jaybone that Lindsey was texting her because Jaybone told Lindsey that Lilith was faking, that she was wasting her time sending those messages, and that Lilith had no intentions of "getting right with the Lord". Lindsey sent the messages anyway. A month later, Lindsey learned that Lilith had been found dead from a combination of a heart attack and a drug overdose.

Though her living arrangements and involvement with Jaybone had changed, Lindsey's devotion to church had not. She still attended church faithfully and sought to be even more involved. While in church one Sunday, Lindsey noticed a man in the back of the church praising the Lord. He was tall with caramel skin and had a confident bearing and a sincere expression. He was unashamed as he lifted his long arms above his head and tilted his head back. She said to herself, *he's going to be my next husband.*

That Monday it was back to her routine. She met with Jaybone at the hotel after dropping her children off. After their encounter, she didn't say a word. She simply got up, washed off, got dressed and said matter-of-factly, "I'm leaving now." Jaybone laid there and said, "you treating me like a nigga. I know you don't love me anymore." For the first time he looked like a child – not the towering, unhinged man that he was. A single tear fell from his eye. She didn't respond. The Lord had answered her prayers. That was the last day she had any sexual desires for Jaybone.

Thirty days had passed and he did not respond to the petition for divorce, so it was time for her to go back to court in Atlanta. "Why do you keep going back to Atlanta?" Her mother asked. Lindsey and her mom were in the kitchen preparing Friday's dinner. She had asked her mother to pick up the children from school because she wouldn't be back in time.

She said, "I still have appointments I must go to." She kept her responses short and sweet, remembering that she had made a promise to herself not to disclose her plans for divorce this time. This is something she had to do all her own. She drove the 3 hours to Atlanta alone, kept company by a few Gospel CDs. She had driven Highway 75 more times than she could count, so the ride was quick and effortless and for the most part, uneventful. When Lindsey arrived at the courthouse, her court-appointed lawyers explained to her that since this was done by publication, a child support order could not be enforced. Lindsey's face remained stoic as she nodded and said she understood. After the lawyer went over the details, he gave the paperwork to the judge, who read the rights of divorce and granted Lindsey a divorce decree.

When she walked out of the courtroom, both jubilated and solemn, she was welcomed with dozens of missed calls from her mother. "I've been calling you to check on you why didn't you answer!?" Her mother was hysterical when Lindsey finally returned her call.

"I couldn't answer my phone because I was in court."

"*Court?* She said dumbfoundedly. "Court for what?"

"Well momma, I'm divorced."

"Divorced! Why didn't you tell me? Why you go through that all by yourself?"

"I didn't go through it by myself. God was with me the whole time, and He told me this was between He and I, that's why I couldn't tell a soul. But I'm on my way back."

On April 6, 2011, Jaybone and Lindsey were officially divorced. This time she sent a mass text to her family and friends, informing them that she had finally gone through with the divorce; and of course, she was flooded with, "why didn't you tell me," or "when did you do it?" She provided the same reason that she'd given her mother. She still hadn't told Jaybone though. She decided to wait until the jubilation wore off and it was the right time. She asked him to meet her in an open area because she had to give him something. They met at a car wash, and she handed him a copy of the divorce decree from her window.

"What's this?" He asked condescendingly.

"We are divorced," she said. He took his copy and they drove off. He called her with a ton of questions concerning how she got a divorce if he wasn't involved or if he hadn't signed any papers. She explained it to him the best she could and ended the conversation before it escalated. He got angry and called her several times before realizing that she was serious about leaving him alone.

Lindsey spent her newfound freedom absorbed in prayer, studying her Word, and focusing on her children. When they weren't with their father, she spent weekends going on outings with them instead of fighting with Jaybone or summoning the evidence for his many indiscretions. The Lord also began waking her in the middle of the night again to deposit a word in her soul; she didn't fight it this time. She just prayed and wrote. She even started back writing her book, feeling that the divorce was a suitable culmination.

A few months later, her and her children were in church, and after the service, a young lady came up to her and said, "My brother wants to know if you can twist his hair."

"Well, who is your brother?"

"He goes to Antioch; his name is Ray."

"Oh, ok." (Lindsey still didn't know who he was). "You can give him my number and he can call me when he is ready."

"Okay, thank you."

"You're welcome." A few days later, she received a phone call. "Hello, can I speak to Lindsey?" His voice was sweet, honest, and had the faint raspiness of a seasoned singer.

"This is she."

"This is Ray, Nene's brother. She told me you do hair and I wanted to know if you can twist mine?"

"Ok, it will have to be any day in the evening or on Saturday because I work during the day."

"Okay, that's fine," he agreed.

"I have to come to you and my children will be with me, will that be okay?"

Without hesitation, he responded, "That's fine."

"Okay, where do you live?"

"9152 Vibe Ave."

Ray gave the complicated directions to his house, and with unexpected butterflies, Lindsey decided it'd be best for him to just text her the address. With that, the two perfect strangers ended their 2-minute phone call. Friday arrived, and after picking up her children from school, they headed to Ray's house. She shampooed and adorned his hair with small and meticulous comb twists. They had very little conversation, and he was polite to her and her children. Once she finished his hair, they left. About 3 weeks later, he called her to make another appointment. After finishing his hair this time, she received a call from him while driving home asking her to take her and her kids out to eat.

"No thank you," she politely declined, "we're going through a divorce, and I'm not ready to date yet."

"I just wanted to take ya'll out to eat," he replied with a tinge of discontent, "but okay, whenever you're ready I'll be here," and they got off of the phone.

Jaybone had been calling and texting Lindsey, leaving obscene messages on her phone. One day she answered because he had called to pick up their children, but she refused because his behavior had been too inappropriate. He had been belligerent, angry, and he had no self-control. Not only did she refuse to let them see their father in this condition, she refused to let them speak to him at all. Lindsey only wanted peace for her children, and she was willing to fight for it. "If you don't let me see my kids, I am going to drive up and down Sherrill Blvd until I find your job and kill you." He had been loud but earnest, and she was quiet and shaken. When she dropped her children off that day, she told the office staff that their dad was not allowed to take them out of school if he happened to come up there. As she was leaving the school, she ran into Jaybone who was causing a scene. He cursed anyone in his path and made proclamations that his bitter ex-wife had maliciously refused to allow him to see his children. Someone in the office staff had called the police who came over and diffused the situation. He encouraged Lindsey to file an order of protection. When she arrived at the Family Justice Center, Jaybone and Willow, the woman who had had an affair with Jaybone and who had been a helpful friend to Lindsey, were already on the elevator. "We beat you to it," he said cynically, "Imma tell them you pulled yo gun out on her."

"That's a lie and you know it," she replied resolutely.

"Yeah, you about to pay now." She didn't say a word as they got off the elevator as he and Willow proceeded to the window first. "We're here to file an order of protection against her," he said clumsily. Lindsey held her lip in and tightened her jaw, a homemade contraption to stifle her tears. The receptionist handed him a stack of papers and told him to have a seat and fill them out.

"I want to file a restraining order against him." If Lindsey hadn't been on the verge of tears, the receptionist may have believed that she was a part of some sick joke; instead, she brought Lindsey behind the counter and took her to another room. The tears that had been brimming below the surface, expelled into a flood of anger. She called her mom and told her what had happened and that she was at the Family Justice Center along with Jaybone and Willow.

"He's telling them that I pulled my gun out on Willow and that's a lie momma, he's lying!"

"Lindsey, I need you to calm down and stop all that crying. All that praying you do in the morning with your prayer warriors, you betta get yoself together and call them and y'all start praying." Netta was a tall, graceful, and hearty woman who enthralled everyone that she met. She served as the queen of hospitality within the family and had a gregarious and fun-loving bearing that put people at ease. With Lindsey though, she was firm and sagacious and accepted nothing but Lindsey's best – this sometimes presented as her being demanding and oppressive, silently seeing Lindsey as a little extension of herself. But mostly it was because she had played both mother and father to Lindsey, oscillating between the two with a rigid confidence. As mother, she was indulgent but strict. As father, she was courageous and affirming. Today she was both. She couldn't bear seeing her daughter being brought to her knees, but she also knew that she couldn't be the one to pick her up either. Lindsey got off the phone with her mom and texted her prayer warriors to get on the line. Whoever was able to call in got on the line, and they started praying immediately. The receptionist at the Justice Center came in the room and went over the paperwork. She said, "Well he doesn't have a case against you because what he was doing was classified as retaliation, and the officer at the school who witnessed the incident notified us that you were coming; so we will send over a request to the judge to grant you a PPO in your favor."

That same night, Lindsey, her mom, and her children went to a revival at Ray's church. Pastor Carmen

Leach was the visiting pastor and had finished preaching and was getting ready to close out. "We're getting ready to go," Pastor Leach said while looking in Lindsey's direction. The look on Lindsey and Netta's face communicated that she had wanted Pastor Leach to stay. That she wasn't finished that evening. "Woman of God, you keep messing with me. I was trying to leave here, but I got to be obedient to God," she started. "Come here," she said while walking down from the pulpit as Lindsey walked up to her. She said, "You just went through something tragic on today, but God is getting ready to vindicate you. Don't worry about what they said because everything is going to turn around in your favor. Be I not a prophet of God." She began speaking prophetically to Lindsey, bringing her to her knees as her mother broke out into a vigorous praise. Church let out, and Ray came over to them, first hugging Netta and then Lindsey. He asked if they wanted dinner from the fellowship hall. Lindsey said, "No," but her children belted out a famished, "Yes."

"Tell them Ray said to fix y'all something to go," he said, "I'm paying for it." They came back with the food and he walked them outside to their car.

"Lindsey did you tell anybody what happen today?" Netta said.

"No momma, I hadn't talked to anybody. Nobody knew but me, you, them, and God."

"You know that wasn't nobody but the Lord," her mother said.

"Yeah, I know," she replied.

That next day Saturday, Lindsey and her children traveled to Atlanta for their doctor's appointment. That night she slept at her son Malik's house – after graduating, he and his cousin got a place in Atlanta – and as she was getting ready to turn out the lights and sleep, her soul spoke to her and said, "That was the guy you were talking about." She sat straight up as she saw Ray's face flash before her when she had said *he's gonna be my next husband*, at the beginning of the year. She sat there with her mouth wide open in amazement. *Oh My God, I did his hair and everything, and I didn't even know that was him*! She turned the lights off. That night she slept well.

"If you ask me, I'm ready." That Sunday morning, she sent a message that would have been ambiguous to most but was undoubtedly clear to the both of them.

Two days later Ray called her and said, "I got your message. So, you're ready, huh?"

She chuckled and said, "Yeah, I believe I am."

He said, "I was in church when I got your text, and was like, who is this? As I kept looking at the text and number, I finally remembered it was you." She blushed for the first time in what seemed to have been a century. "I showed my cousin and said, "Look, look it's her!"

They began having long conversations on the phone like two teenagers. They learned about each other's past, they discussed their shared interests, and they explored the goals that they had in common. Sometimes they'd talk so long that Lindsey found herself awake in the morning dressed in last night's clothes, peeling the phone off of her ear. She had a busy schedule with work, school, and being a mother. She had finally enrolled in college for nursing, and the day she received her school ID, she sobbed and thanked the Lord for her being able to start this goal. Whenever she tried enrolling previously, Jaybone often acted as a hindrance, refusing to help with the kids while she attended classes.

Ray had started visiting her church more, and Jada noticed him interacting with her mother. She would write notes to her mom asking: *the man who hugged you, do you think he is going to marry you? Do you think you and him won't fight? Are you going to tell my father? Do you think he is going to love you forever and take care of you? If you and him marry, can I be the flower girl and get a pet?* This shocked Lindsey. Not only because her eight-year-old daughter was asking these pointed questions, but also because she had realized how much the pain of her previous marriage had been seeped into her memory. Lindsey told Ray that she did not want to argue in front of her children. "But you know we will have arguments and disagreements," he said with his trademark sincerity and self-assuredness. "It's about how we handle them, and they need to know that we will not be perfect and that we can disagree and still love each other. I'm not going to be fake." Lindsey agreed, and for the first time, she felt a comfortable silence.

"I love you." The words seem to just fall out of his mouth. Pure. Concise. Heart-felt. Lindsey sat quietly on the other end of the phone. She would have shed a tear had she not been so caught off guard. Her stomach tightened and her breathing was dense. She did not have to say it back – their friendship had blossomed organically into something more real, more grown-up. "It's not a church love either. I *really* love you."

With effort, her lips finally said, "I don't think it's love. I think you're lusting."

He said with assurance, "don't tell me how I feel, I know I love you." Lindsey was thinking to herself; *how could this man love me? We've never kissed, held hands, or had any sexual encounters.*

She didn't say she loved him back, she simply said, "thank you, I'm in like with you." A few weeks passed, and Ray told Lindsey that she was his girl.

"Oh, you telling me I'm your girl?"

"Sure is, because God said you are going to be my wife."

"No God didn't tell you that."

"He told me the day I seen you at Mount Moriah when you were with your kids. I said to my friend May, 'Who is that because that's my wife,' May said, 'boy everybody your wife.' 'Nawl, that's her, she's the one.'" He then went on to tell her, "I came outside and said hi and you were looking all mean telling your kids to come on."

Lindsey laughed and said, "I was going through something, don't pay any attention to my facial expressions."

"I would have never known you were going through anything because you walked with your head up and I just saw a strength about you."

"Well thank you," Lindsey said. "Now back to this wife thing, I'm not so sure about that."

"Just wait and see; it's going to happen because one thing I don't do is play about God."

"Okay, we'll see," she said. "But I'm not a girl so don't refer to me as your girlfriend, I'll be your lady friend. And you're not a boy so I will address you as my man friend."

"Okay," he chuckled.

One day Ray took Lindsey to meet his father and he introduced her as his girlfriend. This wasn't the same introduction that she had experienced with Jaybone. "I'm not your girlfriend," Lindsey said matter-of-factly.

Ray replied, "Oh you're serious?"

"Sure am," she retorted.

He smiled and said, "Well daddy this is my lady friend, Lindsey."

"Nice to meet you, beautiful" his daddy said. "I like her. Let me tell you something about my son," he continued, "You don't have to worry about him cheating on you, and you don't have to worry about him hitting you." Lindsey sighed with relief at this. Ray's father spoke with an easy reverence as if they were in a preliminary meeting before getting married the next day. It didn't hurt that he had mentioned to Ray that there was something special about her.

They went back to Ray's house. Lindsey sat on the couch watching TV while he made them a meal. After they ate, he sat at the table with his quartet music on low and started sketching. She drifted off to sleep, and when she woke up hours later, Ray hadn't been in the living room. She found herself in a panic, studying the room frantically, feeling as if she were reliving a nightmare. (With Jaybone, she would wake up and he'd be gone during the midnight hours). "Ray!?" She called out distraughtly.

"What's wrong? I'm right here," he replied as he came out of his bedroom.

"Oh, I thought you left."

"Why would I do that?" Lindsey felt the foreign feeling of security. She was surprised at how much she believed him. "I'm not going to leave you. You fell asleep, so I let you rest, and I came here to lie down."

"Well my ex-husband used to leave me when I fell asleep."

"Well I'm not him, so you don't have to worry about that." With that, she continued watching TV in perfect peace.

The following week, Lindsey received a call back about a townhouse she'd been interested in. She met with the owner to tour the place, which was perfect for her and her children. A few days later, the owner called and told her she had been approved. She had prayed for this, had let the Lord guide her, and she received a timely and much needed blessing. Unfortunately, evil must have still been lurking because somehow Jaybone learned of Lindsey dating someone and was irate at this idea though he had a girlfriend himself. Scarlet, his girlfriend and the woman who had been at the center of the chaos that earned Lindsey a gnash to the head, called their son Malik and told him that his dad was out of control, saying he was going to kill Lindsey and Ray and then kill himself. Malik called his mom and told her his dad said he was going to kill her and Ray on site if he saw them together. She called Ray and told him that they had to stop dating.

"Why?" Is all he could muster. He had spent every waking day deciding how he would propose to her. What place. What time. The mood. The words. Everything. She explained what was going on and told him that she didn't want to see anything happen to him and that she didn't want him to be caught in the middle of her issues with her ex-husband. "Oh no, that's not going to happen. I'm not scared of him. We're going to pray about this right now. God told me you are my wife and I will not let you go." Ray began to pray, and afterwards, Lindsey thanked him and they got off of the phone. They continued their relationship, and he started talking more about marriage. "This can't be real," Lindsey would often say.

"Can you please stop saying this can't be real because this is real," he'd reply.

It was Christmas season, and they were rehearsing for a play at church. At one of the rehearsals, Ray approached Netta and asked her for permission to marry her daughter. Though her instinct was to wrap her arms around him, to rejoice at the prospect of her daughter's happiness; she responded with a dubious aloofness. She found his eyes and told him squarely that her daughter had been through a lot and that she didn't want to see her hurt anymore. After that, he went over to Lindsey and told her he had just asked her mother for permission to marry her.

"But you didn't ask me." Lindsey said, a touch of sass in her voice.

He said, "I'm doing this the right way. I had to get permission first. It's coming."

Lord, if this is who you sent for me, let everything happen smoothly, and if he's not, please remove him from my life. She talked to God with desperation. It seemed as if in these last years He was truly her best friend. She petitioned him like her life dependent on it, because it did; she could not afford another Jaybone situation. *This can't be real,* she thought. *Oh, I forgot. Let me stop saying that.*

It was time for Lindsey and the kids to move into their new townhouse. Ray helped her move in and helped drive to Atlanta to get her furniture, which had been in storage. They'd only been dating a few months, and she wasn't quite ready for him to be in her children's life; so, she kept their encounters at his place. She also wanted to make sure they had time to grieve the divorce even though they'd been separated for years prior.

One day while visiting Ray, she came across a porn DVD. She didn't ask any questions. She simply took the tape and broke it in half.

"Why'd you do that? That wasn't mine. That was my cousin's."

"Well the fact that you had it in your house is what bothers me. I don't like porn and I will not tolerate pornography."

He started laughing saying, "now I gotta buy my cousin another DVD."

Lindsey said, "I'm not laughing, I'm serious." Lindsey was never fond of porn as it had been a problem in her 1st marriage for which she refused to partake - the idea of a fantasy possibly ruining a future sickened her.

Chapter Eight: Mending the Pieces

Gracie's funeral had been a somber tribute. She was Lindsey's younger cousin and was 18 when she passed. Her death had been unexpected, sending a jolting shock through the family. And like many funerals, it was also time to bring the family together, a sobering reminder of what's important. After the funeral, Lindsey and her family gathered around aunt Glory, Gracie's mother's house, as they often did for special occasions. She had been a single mother with three other children and decided to declutter her home to leave room for her grief. She told her sisters and nieces that they could have whatever they wanted under the piles of books, clothes, and other belongings. Jada, being an avid reader at seven years old, went through the box and picked up the books *Children and Divorce* and *How to Love a Nice Guy*. Everyone looked with ecstatic faces and Lindsey's aunt

Glory said, with a smile on her face, "Oh, oh, I believe God is trying to tell you something from her giving you those books." Lindsey read both books as they were a help to her in the rebuilding process.

On a visit to Ray's house one day, he began to serenade her with the song, "Never Felt This Way" by Brian McKnight. *"There will never come a day. You'd ever hear me say. That I want and need to be without you. I want to give my all."* She had never heard of the song; all she knew was that it moved her, making her feel both adored and worthy. He then gave her a ring and said, "This is not a wedding ring, this was my mother's ring; and I want you to have it because I promise it will turn into a wedding ring." Lindsey could not stop smiling at the prospect of his sharing something so pure with her. She was even more surprised because they hadn't had any sexual encounters yet. *He must be for real about me*, she thought. They vowed to remain abstinent until marriage, which was difficult for Lindsey because her and Jaybone had sex two or three times a day throughout their marriage. Whenever things became too heated amongst her and Ray, they'd separate. During a phone conversation, they began talking about wedding dates, and he asked her when she wanted to get married.

"Well you haven't asked me to marry you yet."

He said, "I told you it was coming."

"Lindsey said, "Oh okay, well not November."

"Not August," Ray said. "How about September?"

"September? September is good. Okay now what day?"

He said, "How about the 15th?"

Lindsey said, "Sounds good."

After months of their visits being limited to Ray's house, he began to visit Lindsey. One night, in a conversation about the wedding, Ray did something that left her in tears. He told her how his mom, who had passed, would have been so pleased with Lindsey and how she had told him that his ex-wife was not the one for him. As he went on, Lindsey's mind went back to her also being told that her first marriage should have never taken place either.

"Wow!" she said, as her eyes welled with tears.

"What is it?" Ray said.

"The Lord just showed me that He blocked that day on September 15, 1997. The day that Jaybone and I attempted to get married because *He* had already preserved that day for us, 15 years later." They both sat there chilly with disbelief. Their faith had solidified in that moment, making them realize that marriage was the only choice for them.

Their relationship had progressed to a point of comfort amongst the children, well, at least it had with Jada. Lindsey and Ray were sitting on the couch watching T.V. when Jada described her time with her father over the weekend.

"Did y'all have fun? What did you do?

"We had fun momma, I was with my two brothers too," Jada said. Lindsey sat dumbfounded as her two sons were much too old, and too cool, to play with Jada. "You know Willow, she got two sons."

"Okay baby that's good, I'm glad y'all had fun." Jada went upstairs to her room as Lindsey's heart shattered and her eyes welled with tears. Later she would learn that Jaybone fathered Willow's children because she wanted more and he was being a good friend.

Ray pulled her into him, and she lay tucked under his arms like a child in need of protection. "Let it out," he cried as he gripped her tighter. "Let it out."

Not too many months after their conversation about wedding dates, Ray told her that he had something to talk to her about. Her heart fell to her gut. *Could he be breaking up with me?* He came over to her house and asked if they could go upstairs to her room. *I knew it was too good to be true.* She sat on the bed, and he stood up. "You know how I feel about you," he started. "I see how you like to keep your house and take care of your kids, and I like that about you." She trembled as he dropped on one knee. "I want to be a part of y'alls life. Will you marry me?"

With her hand over her mouth, she shrieked, "Yes, yes!" He kissed her and placed the ring on her finger. "I thought you were going to call off the relationship," she chuckled.

"Why would you think that?"

"Well, the adjustment of my children getting used to this, I didn't know if that was getting to you."

"I can handle that," he said. "Look, when I take you, I'm taking your kids too, and they'll come around. We'll keep praying," he assured her and embraced her lovingly.

Even in her bliss, she knew she had to break the news of their engagement to her children. Jada had been gitty and preoccupied with ensuring her role as flower girl, but she knew which child would take it the hardest. Jordan had only known his family, and that family did not include a tall fair-skinned man named Ray. When she finally mustered up the courage to tell him, he fell to the floor and cried. She grabbed her son, held him, and they cried together, explaining to him that it was officially over with her and their dad, and there were no hopes of them getting back together. She explained to him that it was time for her to be happy and she believed that God had sent that person for her. Though receptive, Jordan was still hurt.

Lindsey and Ray continued with their wedding planning; it was the same ceremony that she had planned in 1998 for Jaybone and her after they exchanged vows. The colors remained a fall symphony of chocolate and ivory with lilac instead of burnt orange. The score and the wedding party remained with a few additions from Ray. Their wedding planning was a pleasure to the both of them, they were in perfect harmony as they designed a ceremony fit for a couple who had fought for love and won. This was amplified by the fact that neither of them had a wedding in their previous marriages. As soon as Lindsey would start wedding planning, Jaybone and she would get into a horrible fight; and she would postpone it.

It was time for the wedding. Lindsey was overjoyed with the idea that this time when she sent a mass message to her family and friends, it would be to invite them to her love story instead of engaging them in her despair. They came from Memphis, Atlanta, and Detroit to witness their joyous occasion. When Lindsey's friends came over to their house, they were surprised to see an extra bed.

Her friend Meka commented, "Who sleeps in that bed?"

"That's where Ray sleeps."

"Girl, y'all were serious!"

"Uh...yeah," Lindsey smiled. Mount Moriah FBH was adorned with laced pews and large vases designed in chocolate and ivory and overflowed with exotic flowers. The men wore chocolate suits, and the women wore silky chocolate dresses. Lindsey's cousin, Colonel Pastor James Kirkwood, officiated the ceremony. In his booming baritone voice, he engaged their guests in the ceremony while also delivering an eloquent and tailored tribute to their love. Lindsey was a princess. She wore a studded crown and a lilac gown reminiscent of Cinderella. The ceremony had been full of romantic surprises and heartfelt singing, culminating with Ray surprising her with a serenade of "Never Felt This Way".

After the wedding and hours of dancing at the reception, the two went on a one-week cruise to the Bahamas for their honeymoon and returned to start their life together as husband and wife.

That Friday, Lindsey, Ray, Jordan, and Jada were preparing to take Lindsey's father to the bus station; he had stayed in Knoxville to take care of the children during their honeymoon. When they returned home, Jordan immediately got out of the car and slammed Ray's door. "You didn't have to slam the door like that," Ray said.

"I didn't slam your door," he seethed and pushed Ray. As Jada got out of the truck, she heard their altercation and witnessed another push. Jordan took off running around the corner to his brother Malik's house while Ray stood fuming.

It seemed to have come out of nowhere, a speeding car came down their street with the driver cursing and threatening Ray, urging him to pick out a suit because he would kill him and send him in a body bag with his parents for touching his son. It was Jaybone. "Dad, dad, he didn't touch me. He didn't touch me!" Jordan cried.

Ray looked at Jaybone and said, "Oh, you got that" and walked in the house. Ray stayed downstairs and talked to Lindsey's dad about what had transpired. Lindsey went upstairs to change clothes for the church service they'd be attending after taking her father to the bus station.

"Don't you eva put yo' hands on my brother…!" While Lindsey was upstairs, downstairs sounded like a wrestling match. Harsh words escalating into a tug-of-war between Ray and Malik, who had come over unannounced. It only went downhill when Malik's girlfriend, Tori, and another friend jumped into the fight. Lindsey peeled Tori off of Ray as her dad broke up the altercation between him and Malik.

"Call the police!" Lindsey hollered. "Call the police!" Lindsey made a futile attempt to calm Ray down as her younger children sobbed uncontrollably upstairs. It was a disaster, and it had only been a week since they exchanged vows.

"I guess you want me to leave now?" Ray said to Lindsey. She didn't answer him, she just looked at him with tears rolling down her face. The police showed up and Lindsey explained everything. They asked if Lindsey and Ray wanted to press charges, and they both said, "no" though Lindsey did want an order of protection on her ex-husband and her son. The officers gave her a report number, and they left.

"Are you sure you want to take out an order of protection on your son?" Ray asked.

"I have to," Lindsey said. It tore her heart to pieces. *How can you choose this man over your own flesh and blood? You've only known him for a year,* she thought. In her mind, it had really been too good to be true. Before she became undone, she was reminded of the Biblical verse, "For this cause shall a man leave father and mother, and cleave to his wife: and they twain shall be one flesh...what therefore God hath joined together, let not man put asunder." They went ahead and took her dad to the Greyhound bus station and continued to church; Pastor Marvin Sapp was the visiting speaker. The walls of the church reverberated with praise. The pews were filled with shouts and screams of "hallelujah", and the choir bellowed songs of inspiring worship. Others sat patiently waiting for Marvin to take the podium. Ray and Lindsey sat in silence. Lindsey was numb and he was consumed with feelings of retaliation. Ray was diabetic, and during the altercation, he thought he had broken his toe.

The truck ride home had been one of pure silence; and when they returned home, they were met with the hollow remnants of the chaos they'd endured that evening. Instead of melting into the couch as they'd done after many long nights, Lindsey swiftly left the house and went to the store to clear her head.

"I thought you were not coming back." Hours had passed before Lindsey returned home. "I thought it was going to be over." Ray's voice was solemn. *There's no way she's going to stay with me over her son,* he thought.

Lindsey said, "Well I thought *you* would have left. I figured you would have said, 'I don't have to stay here and be in all this baby daddy drama.'" They both forced a laugh.

Ray grabbed Lindsey and said, "Look, yes I'm angry, I'm really angry, but I love you and your kids. I know it's not their fault. I'm not trying to take their dad's place, but I will be here for them as a father figure, a friend, and whatever they need me to be. I'm not going anywhere. We will get through this. I understand you want to file an order of protection on your ex-husband, but are you really sure you still want to go through this with Malik?"

Through tears she said, "He was wrong, and he's grown. I have to teach him. This is killing me Ray!" Ray grabbed her and squeezed her tightly.

Days had passed since the altercation, and Ray and Lindsey were going through the motions. Work. Home. Work. Home. On one particular day, after coming home and taking off his work boots, Lindsey examined his foot. "I think we should go to the emergency room," she said. But Ray refused because he didn't have insurance.

The next day when they got home from work, Lindsey looked at his toe, which had been stabilized with a bandage and Popsicle stick, and it started discoloring. "I don't care what you say, we are going to the emergency room because you are a diabetic and you can't play around with this." Though they went to the hospital, the doctors refused to care for him because he didn't have insurance and the severity of the problem was too costly. So, they went to another hospital. The doctors there took him in, but the outcome was not good. Ray had to have his toe amputated as it was too late to save.

Lindsey sunk into a deep depression. The distance between her and her son as well as her husband losing a toe were both taking a toll on her. Ray noticed the change in her and would often ask if she had spoken to Malik. Lindsey would shake her head, "no," and he would say, "You need to call your son, babe."

"I'm not. Not this time," she said. "He's going to come to me and apologize first."

As the holidays were approaching, she missed her son more; and she found herself talking more and more about not having him near.

"Maybe I should leave so you and your kids can be together and happy again," Ray said.

"Now that ain't nothing but the devil. He's trying to make God out to be a lie. Like you said, we'll get through this," she assured him.

It was December, and with it came Lindsey's birthday. That morning, she woke up to a *Happy Birthday* text that made her day. It was from Malik. She had spent the rest of the day rather simply but marked with a permanent smile. Malik's simple step would be the first toward the healing that was going to take place in the family. Eventually, they would make small talk through sporadic calls and texts. Then one day, Malik came to his mother and apologized for his behavior; they discussed that day, the day of the altercation, and decided to move forward. From that conversation, Lindsey got her children together; and she apologized to them again for keeping them in a dysfunctional household far too long because of her selfish reasons. She explained to her children that now was the time for them to be truly happy. She told them that she believed that it was God that sent Ray for her, for them. She let them know that she would never put them to the side for anyone, but her husband came first according to the Bible, and she wanted them to be included in their happiness as a family. She was not going to allow them, or anyone, to make her feel guilty for being happy after all the hell she had been through. "You all are at the age where you can choose to stay mad and distance yourself, or you can get on board and choose to be happy; it's your choice," she said. "I don't want y'all to feel sorry for your dad either, because he made his choices as well, and y'all can't fix it. It's not y'alls fault."

Malik told his mom that his dad had asked if something was wrong with her because of how small she had gotten – her and Ray were on a strict exercise regime and maintained a healthy diet – and that he hoped she wasn't smoking crack because she had smoked it before. "Boy, ya daddy lying to you cause I ain't neva smoked no crack; I don't know where he got that from!" But in that moment her heart sank, and she began to question the credibility of what she had just heard. *Why would he say that?* Then she remembered the time he had asked her if she wanted to smoke weed when they made a sell at someone's house and how good it had made her feel. "OH MY GOD," she said, "I know he didn't lace that weed with crack."

Lindsey knew becoming a blended family would be an adjustment, especially for her children; but Ray and she were willing to pray through the situation. Not too long after Lindsey and Malik mended their relationship, Malik asked Ray if he could talk to him. Though Ray didn't go into great detail about their conversation – he promised that he would keep what they'd discussed in confidence – he did share with her that Malik apologized for the incident and that he was grateful to be back in his mother's life and that he was also grateful for Ray being in his siblings' life and for his being a Godly man. "How could I say I love your mom and hate what belongs to her? I love all y'all," he told Malik. Although more work was needed; this was God continuing to answer their prayers.

Chapter Nine: The Birthing

Ray's leg had begun to swell from long hours of working, and this was augmented by his working a second job to pay child support from his previous marriage. Lindsey asked him to quit the second job because of his health issues, but he refused. To make matters worse, his foot had been progressively going downhill, and his doctor recommended that he stop all employment and apply for disability again. "I don't normally do this because I believe a man should work, but I really care about you Ray, so I will write a letter for you to take to disability because I don't see you working on this foot without losing it." His doctor's words cut like a knife to Ray's pride. It killed him that he would be unemployed and unable to provide for his family, but he also knew that this would be a matter of life and death. That his healing and physical presence surpassed any amount of money. "Are y'all going to be able to make it financially until you find out from disability?"

"We have no choice," Lindsey said.

On the ride home, Lindsey told Ray, "God will provide." Ray put his notices in on both of his jobs, and he suffered another toe amputation.

Lindsey was back in a place of torturous guilt, thinking, "if we hadn't caused this fight, he wouldn't be in this situation." The Lord spoke to her again, telling her that even in what seemed to be a bad situation, He allowed it to happen.

Ray seemed to be doing well on the outside. He wasn't taking any medication, and he wasn't seeing any doctors; but on the inside is where the problem lay. Ray himself seemed to be doing fine, but because he had not been followed by a doctor to receive continuous monitoring, there was an underlying problem. He may have suffered a diabetic coma.

"This is that in sickness and in health part you say in your marriage vows," said Lindsey. But Ray wasn't trying to hear it; all he knew was that a man was supposed to take care of his family. He went to oxygen therapy five days a week and sometimes on Saturday to help with his foot. On the days he had energy, he would have a full course meal ready when Lindsey and the children came home from work and school. The house would be cleaned, and he would help Jada with her homework. He cared for their infant grandbaby while her parents worked. But he was still out of work, and that fact depressed him. Lindsey would often thank him and remind him how grateful she was for his helping her with their home in spite of his condition. As his foot began to heal, he talked about going back to work; but Lindsey wasn't convinced that it was a good idea. Thank God she did because another setback came. Somehow, Ray developed a diabetic ulcer on the bottom of his foot which required another surgery to remove the infected bone. While in the hospital, they discovered that he developed kidney issues due to an allergic reaction to the contrast dye from an MRI, but his doctor was able to attack the problem before it caused any major damage.

On a Monday morning, after having gotten fired from her job, she went to the unemployment office and applied for unemployment and then went to the Department of Human Services and applied for food stamps and health insurance. When she went inside the crowded food stamp office, and saw a sea of desperate faces, she turned around and walked toward the door to leave out. As she got to the door, her intuition told her, "lose your pride; this is not your end." *A temporary setback is a setup for a permanent blessing.* She turned around and got in line. When she got back home, she told Ray, "I'm not used to going without stuff. I had it all. My mother had it all for me. This is going to be hard."

He said, "Well I didn't have everything, but I couldn't tell. You gotta stop thinking like that. We just have to trust God, Lindsey." She was beginning to see that God was breaking her pride. He was bringing her to a place where she had to increase her faith and trust solely on Him. Ray continued to go to therapy and Lindsey would have sporadic hair clients.

It was time for Lindsey's appointment at the food stamp office, and on her way there, her tire blew. She called her son to come get her and switch cars because she didn't have time to wait for him to change her tire. Lindsey made it to her appointment, and while in the back with the caseworker, she asked if she needed any repairs on her vehicle. Lindsey said, well, "I did have a blow out on the way here, and I believe something is wrong with my tire."

"Well, we have this program that will help you with repairs, but you won't be eligible for monthly cash payments if you get approved."

"I did not apply for cash payments," Lindsey said. The caseworker then told Lindsey all that was needed for approval. Lindsey went to a mechanic and got an estimate for repairs. She submitted the estimate and the other information to her caseworker, and within a few days, she received a call stating that she had been approved and that a debit card would be arriving soon. She received a Visa debit card with $2,100 to have repairs done on her car. Lindsey knew that was nothing but God working things out in her favor.

When she received her unemployment letter, she learned that she'd be getting the maximum amount. She continued to pay her tithes and offerings, staying faithful in the church. Ray and she also continued to read their word and pray. As she was learning to adapt to this new arrangement, she began to think of the verse, "Let us not become weary in doing good, for at the proper time we will reap a harvest if we do not give up" (NIV). Because of their obedience in doing what was right, God was still providing for them right when they needed it. Someone would come up to either one of them and place money in their hands; someone would give them a check; or someone would even ask for a utility account number so they could pay a bill. Other times, someone would call them and say, "I'm by your house, come to the door. I got something for y'all." And sometimes people would simply take care of their bill at a restaurant. In Lindsey's mind, this reminded her of the Biblical verses, Philippians 4:19, "But my God shall supply all your needs according to his riches in glory by Christ Jesus," and Proverbs 18:22, "Whoso findeth a wife findeth a good thing, and obtaineth favor of the Lord." (KJV). In this trying season, she was truly learning to understand the concept of faith and trust in God.

It was August, and Lindsey had gone to T.D. Jakes' International "Women Thou Art Loose" conference in Atlanta with a few other ladies. It was time for offering, and the ladies in Lindsey's pew methodically passed the silver offering plate with gratuitous smiles and affirming head nods. Once it came to Lindsey, she neatly handed it to the usher who was set to walk away when Lindsey was handed an envelope. She took the envelope, and as she scooted down the bench to place it in the usher's hands, a woman quietly said to her, "no, that's for you." Lindsey hugged the mysterious woman and thanked her. She didn't even look in the envelope, she just put it in her purse; and they went back into praise and worship. When that session of the conference was over, she met up with the rest of the ladies to go back to the Marta station. As they were waiting for the train to come, Lindsey opened the envelope and it read, *The Lord placed it in my heart to give you this. Please receive it in the name of Christ! It's already alright - God Bless You!* She opened it up and it was $100. To some it may not seem like much, but for Lindsey it was the perfect blessing, a reminder that she had not been forgotten. So, she did what she knew how to do; she started praising God right there in the Marta station and blessed her sister in Christ with a portion of what she had received.

She couldn't get to the hotel fast enough before calling her husband and sharing her blessing. Once she returned home, Ray and she discussed how the Lord was still making ways even in the midst of their struggles. They also baffled about how they hadn't thrown in the towel on each other, how they were still able to laugh and enjoy each other, and most importantly, how they were still able to praise the Lord together. In their eyes, it had truly been the power of God holding them together.

Through laughs and shares on that couch after the conference, Ray had a confession for Lindsey. He had still been battling his obsession with pornography.

"I already knew you were," Lindsey said, "but instead of arguing with you about it after I already spoke to you, I went into prayer and asked God to convict you and remove that desire from you."

"Well I've been praying too, and I don't want to hurt you or displease God. I got free on Sunday."

"Well I'm happy for you babe, she said." The old Lindsey would have cursed him, searching and destroying phones. As she matured in her walk with God, she learned how to fight in the spirit instead of in the flesh. She knew he was sent by God, *so why throw him away over what only God can fix?*

October arrived and the family, including Netta, were preparing to travel to Lindsey's hometown Detroit for her cousin Barbie's 50th birthday celebration, a much needed get-away. They arrived on a Friday to parlay with family and friends before the party on Sunday. Barbie was a fair-skinned, fully-framed woman with a loud voice and an even larger laugh. Her hair was dyed a golden blond and cropped short - either slicked to her head or curled in numerous patterns. She always had a quip or compliment at the ready. She also happened to be the family's cook and party thrower; so, this event, her 50th birthday, glistened with a sparkle that only she could muster. Lindsey fully enjoyed herself. Dancing, eating, and catching up with her relatives. During the party, her much adored aunt Jackie, with her keen intuition, asked Ray if he was okay. He responded that he was fine, but Lindsey would learn differently.

"Is the air on?" It was October, but Ray had been sweating profusely in the passenger side of their truck as they hit the highway that Monday to return to Knoxville.

"Yeah, do you need me to turn it up?" Netta asked.

"Yes please," he said.

A few minutes later, Ray said, "it's hot in here. I can't breathe."

"I put the air on high; let me roll down the windows."

As Lindsey was driving, her mom looked back at Ray as he cried, "I can't breathe!" and broke out into a sweat.

"Pull over, Lindsey! Pull over!" Netta screamed.

"You want me to pull over in the middle of the road? There's no exit!" Lindsey said. Lindsey looked up and saw that the next exit was a rest stop. She was going about 100 miles per hour when she turned into the rest area. She jumped out and ran to the back side where Ray was sitting. His eyes were wide open and he wasn't responding, breathing shallow like a fish out of water gasping for air.

Lindsey hollered, "Ray, Ray don't you die on me! Don't you die on me! *Breathe!*" She hovered over him, forgetting everything she'd learned in the medical industry. Her mind was a fog. All she could do was feel and scream. "Jada, go get somebody," she bellowed, "Momma, call 911!"

"The ambulance is on their way," Netta said. Lindsey finally checked his pulse, which was faint. She kept talking to him and telling him to breathe. She then called their friend and Ray's cousin, Bishop Chris Holloway. As the phone was ringing, she continued to call Ray's name.

"Um, this isn't Ray, this is Bishop," he said puzzledly.

"Bishop, Ray can't breathe, and he's incoherent!"

"What? Put the phone up to his ear." Lindsey put the phone up to Ray's ear as Bishop prayed fervently. As he prayed, Ray began a slow slur that resembled speaking. She took the phone off of his ear and told Bishop that the EMT was there and that they were on their way to the hospital. "Keep me posted," he said.

It took three workers to pull Ray out of the truck and onto the gurney. As they were about to leave, Netta's truck wouldn't start. "Oh no!" Lindsey said, "what is going on?" The fireman came over and gave them a boost, and they were on their way to a hospital in Findley, Ohio. Once they arrived at the hospital, which seemed to be in the middle of nowhere, they learned that they had almost lost Ray in the ambulance. They had to shock his heart back into rhythm because he had gone into kidney failure; his potassium levels were through the roof.

When they rolled Ray into his room, Lindsey took out her blessing oil and anointed his body and began to pray over him. As the days progressed, his numbers were beginning to go back to a normal range. The doctor said his kidneys were looking better and that he didn't need emergency dialysis after all. Lindsey thanked God in her quiet time, believing that her prayers had been answered.

Ray went in for testing, and Netta's Pastor and his wife had driven up from Knoxville, TN to pick her and Jada up so they wouldn't miss any more work or school. *What is the reason for all of this?* She petitioned God. *Elevation. It's the process of elevation.*

Ray and Lindsey were in a transition. It was a spiritual move taking place. They had discussed leaving their current church, and after Ray's scare and the drama surrounding Jaybone, that conversation resurfaced. While she had been battling with the transition, Ray was sure about it. She didn't understand why the move had to happen because she felt as if she was getting what she needed at their current church home. As the two of them would receive confirmation after confirmation that the transition was necessary for their elevation, Lindsey fought it the more. She kept asking God for one more sign. She simply wasn't ready to transition from a place to which she'd grown attached. She would even back out of informing their leaders when they both agreed they would have a talk with them. One night after Bible class, Ray said to Lindsey, "so are we going to talk to them?"

"I'm not ready," she said.

"Well, we're not waiting any longer, I'm going to talk to them." The ride to Mount Moriah was a quiet one. Lindsey weaved a string of explanations in her head, hoping to find the right words that'd let their pastors down easily. Ray thumped the steering wheel in assured anticipation. When they arrived at the church, their pastor met them with a smile that showed his delight in seeing them. That smile relaxed a bit when Ray broke the news about their leaving. As Ray started talking, Lindsey couldn't stop crying.

She finally said, "It's not y'all. Please understand that. Our moving has nothing to do with anyone here or anyone making us mad. This is strictly a spiritual move."

"Let's give it some time," their pastor said. "Let's wait a few months and see how things go before y'all move."

That next day, Ray and Lindsey called Bishop Holloway and asked if they could meet with him and his wife. He agreed, and the four of them went out to meet in a little restaurant in downtown Knoxville. Bishop Holloway was a young, prophetic pastor that was earnest about preaching the truth, saving souls, and was passionate about helping all nationalities through community outreach. After exchanging a few pleasantries, Ray told them that he and Lindsey knew that they were called to be a part of their ministry at Divine Worship Christian Center. He asked them if they were sure this is what the Lord told them to do and if they had spoken to their leaders about it. They simply explained to him that their season was up at their previous church and that they knew the Lord was calling them to transition to his ministry. "I just want to make sure this is done decently and in order," he maintained.

On his third day at the hospital, the doctor came in and said they were released to go home. *There is something about what happens in three days*, she thought. They made it back home safely to Knoxville, and Ray followed up with his nephrologist who explained that at the moment, his kidneys were good, but he didn't foresee him living a long life without dialysis and a kidney transplant due to the damage caused by diabetes.

Lindsey returned to work as a PCA, but she despised it so much that it started to affect her heart. She felt like the Lord was telling her to quit and trust him. *I can't quit*, she thought. *I don't have another job ye*t. Lindsey's faith was being tested, and she had to trust the plan that the Lord had for her. It had gotten to the point that God had to push her to leave. She had found herself in the same situation. It had become a theme in her life. She knew something needed to change, typically a move, she hesitated, but radical circumstances pushed her out of a seat like opponents playing musical chairs.

It was 4:45am when Lindsey arrived at work. The birds were chirping as usual, the sun was on the horizon, but this particular day seemed auspicious. Her coworker handed her a report that stated that almost every patient on her hall was incontinent. She had two deceased bodies that she had to prepare for pick up, and as soon as she received her phone, she had gotten another call that another patient had expired. That did it! Lindsey went in the break room and wrote her resignation letter. She didn't even have a job lined up yet; all she knew was that she had big, ridiculous faith and trust in God. Three days later, she got a call to come in for an interview at a doctor's office and was hired on the spot. *It's just something about three days,* she thought.

Lindsey's faith had once again been renewed. She had a job she enjoyed, a solid relationship with her children, and Ray's health had been improving. Still, there was one aspect of their lives that gave them pause. "We have to stop being afraid and start this new journey." He had been referring to their leaving their church. His voice had the same conviction as it did the day he asked Lindsey to be his girlfriend and as it did when he asked her to be his wife. Mount Moriah had been the church where she first saw Ray, and it was where their bond had been solidified; so, the prospect of leaving frightened them both.

After their church's yearly convention, they officially left and began attending Bishop Holloway's church. It wasn't long before they took the right hand of fellowship and became members. As they continued training into the ministerial calling, it seemed like their tests and trials intensified. There were many conversations that Lindsey had with the Lord asking, "why?" *Because you two have a work to do,* she heard Him say; and "how long?" *Until My Glory comes.* In the years she spent with Jaybone, her life had been painted with agony, abuse, and despair; so, she was anxious for true peace and true happiness and true fulfillment.

During a leadership meeting at their new church, the leaders were asked if there were any issues at home that could possibly affect them in having an effective ministry. As Ray raised his hand and began to speak, Lindsey had a grin on her face, believing that he'd make a joke. "My wife's mouth," he asserted. She and the other members shared laughs and then he said, "no, I'm serious," she then grew agitated and quiet. "I'm done." She became furious! *How dare he embarrass me in front of all of those people,* she thought. Her pride seeped in, threatening to unravel the holy robe that she adorned. After their meeting, she left to go to the ATM and get her tithe, when the Bishop texted her, "I need you to get back here and come see me." After church service, they went home and her husband explained what he was saying.

"Babe," he started, "I first want to apologize for what I said if it made you feel some type of way, but I wasn't saying it like that. I'm not leaving you. I wasn't saying I was done with our marriage, I'm just tired of your mouth. There's been a change in you lately, you've been snapping at everybody, having an attitude, you just haven't been yourself; and every time I ask you what's wrong, you say nothing, and I can't take it anymore."

"Well you were wrong for saying that at church, but if that's what God told you to do, then okay," and she walked away into the bedroom. Lindsey could be stubborn; and after a few days of praying and listening to God, she heard the Lord say, *apologize*. She had only been masking her feelings about her husband's health and their finances. She didn't want to compound his worries with hers, but she didn't know that her worries had been coming out in her attitude. When she wanted to complain, she often thought about how her husband had lost both his parents, and that he had been dealing with health problems; yet he still carried on without complaint. She apologized, and he accepted.

Lindsey and Ray became licensed ministers after serving under Bishop Chris Holloway for one year. They had studied and served diligently, learning more about the work of ministry and giving their first sermon. The church was filled with family and friends who had come to witness their glorious occasion. It brought tears to their eyes as Lindsey felt chosen and honored that God had never left her despite her straying from him.

Ray continued to have his health issues, but they were under control with dialysis, Lindsey's care, and an abundance of faith. The purpose for their pain was finally starting to make some sense. Lindsey and Ray may have been broken separately, but their brokenness somehow found their way to connect them to each other and to create beauty. In their brokenness, they learned how to truly love and submit to one another. While they waited together for the healing of Ray's body or for a new kidney, they vowed to be a force together and to continue to do the work of the Lord. AMEN.

Epilogue/Conclusion

Hi I'm Lindsey, also known as LaQuanda. Thank you for purchasing my book or borrowing it from a friend :). I hope you've enjoyed what you've read and have taken something out of it for yourself or to share with someone you want to help. This book is not to bash anyone but to bring awareness to the hidden domestic violence that takes place daily in homes that "look" like they have it all together. Though my ex-husband turned to the streets for income, he was not solely dependent upon the streets at first. He worked hard, but the streets got the best of him at that time. He made things happen for his family by any means, and I give him credit for that; but that was not the life I wanted to continue to raise our children in.

My goal for this book is to reach as many women as I can to let them know that abuse of any kind is not okay! Yes, some men suffer abuse as well, but not nearly as much as women; so, I decided to focus more on women because of the staggering statistics that prove that we are most likely to be victims, and of course because I AM WOMAN! God did not intend for women to be abused by men. Yes, God does hate divorce and the scripture says, *What God has joined together, let no man separate*, but I still believe that He will give you peace in your decision and provide a way of escape, especially if He didn't orchestrate the marriage. Sometimes we join ourselves with men or women before seeking God. I lost myself trying to save someone else not knowing the effects it would have on my children. *Don't lose yourself in the ring fighting for someone else when you haven't fought for yourself!* No matter how much you think you're hiding it from the children, they see, they hear, they feel, and they remember. They are a part of us. Even after the divorce, my ex-husband still controlled me. I found myself giving in to my children out of fear from his reactions. I found myself rerouting my drive to avoid place where I'd catch him with other women. It wasn't until I regained my self-love and my self-confidence that I took a stand and told myself "no more living in fear of him, no more letting this situation control me." Instead, I began to control the situation. I began to stand up to him and tell him NO! *There was no more compromising my peace, my children's peace.* Although I have some physical wounds, body altercations, and suffer from chronic migraines due to the head trauma that resulted in me becoming medication dependent, when the past visits me, it doesn't consume me. I praise God for letting me make it out. I AM FREE! When I felt in my spirit that the atmosphere he wanted our children in wasn't conducive to their health and growth, I stopped letting them go with him. Yes, it did hurt me knowing that they wanted to be with their dad, but keeping peace in our home was better for us once we finally achieved it.

When I thought I was totally free from my ex-husband, my now husband asks if I still love him because my attitude would change when he came around. I asked him to explain, and he did. From what my actions showed, I was still angry. I was angry at the fact that I felt like he got away free. He hardly helped with support for our children and always hand an excuse as to why. I was made to be the bad parent because I had to do the disciplining as well as loving, and when they were in his presence, it was all fun. He could do something as small as get an ice cream from McDonald's and he's, "father of the year" but would not do anything for months later; meanwhile I was providing a home, paying bills, and providing for our children's wants and needs. Yes, I know it's time spent that matters, but I just wanted him to pay for the hurt he had caused. Then my husband said, "Babe you can't think like that, he is not getting away with anything. The Lord will take care of him." That's when this scripture came to mind: **Romans 12:19: Do not take revenge, my dear friends, but leave room for God's wrath, for it is written: "It is mine to avenge; I will repay," says the Lord (NIV).** After that conversation with my husband, my whole attitude changed about my ex-husband. Free I am; indeed, I am Free.

I believe God used Caucasians in my rebuilding process as well. I grew to hate white women after the affairs my ex-husband had with so many of them, I also grew to despise biracial children. Then the Lord said to me, "what is the difference between white women and black women? They're both women that your husband cheated on you with. So, you can't hate one without hating the other." That's when my heart changed, and it was the Lord that softened it. The very thing or person that you despise will be that very thing or person that God uses to bless you. *Change your posture.* At that time in my life I predominantly worked with Caucasians and had much interactions with Caucasian patients. Even on a no make-up day I often got.... "you are so beautiful; you have a beautiful spirit." Not saying my own race didn't compliment me, but other races said it more. I started saying to myself, "well, maybe I am beautiful if they keep telling me that." I started looking in the mirror and smiling at myself more. I didn't think I was beautiful because something had to be wrong with me to get treated the way I did for so long. Perhaps, I didn't have the right looks? On top of being self-conscious about my lazy eye (I love it now), I often wondered, "Is my body not the right size?" But when I saw the females that my ex-husband cheated on me with, I learned that that possibly couldn't be it.

Ladies, a lot of times when "grown boys" try to break you, it's them who are broken and do not love themselves. They are intimidated by your strength and will try to tear you down instead of helping build you up. When you finally decide to accept that invitation from that man who has found you, do not make him suffer from your past. Make sure you make your requests known to God how you want your mate to be, even down to your sexual desires. Make sure your request is determined upon how *you* need to be when he finds you as well. I will say 95% of my request was answered. When your partner can make love to your mind before they ever make love to you physically, I believe you have something worth fighting for.

Lastly, recognize the signs of abuse and get out. That one hit should not be negotiable; it is intolerable and you must leave. But there are also emotional signs of abuse: jealousy, accusation, blaming, criticizing, threatening, name-calling, denial, and anger are just a few. I am far from perfect in this. I had my share of dirt, and I rendered my share of physical abuse to my ex-husband. But you do know there is a reaction for every action. Although, my reactions were not Godly, they should have been. I felt justified in my behavior because of the way I was being treated. But I was all wrong because I knew the Word of God; I just didn't apply it to my situation. Regardless of what my ex-husband was doing to me, I still should have been the Godly wife that was instructed of me from a Biblical stance at all times, not only when I thought he deserved it. I'm not saying take whatever your abuser delivers, but respond with wisdom and knowledge from the Lord, because ultimately, He is the one that is fighting for you. It was all a part of my process. That's what happens when God is not the head and center of your marriage, or your relationship. When God did not orchestrate the relationship, expect the unexpected.

Get out!!! Stay out!!! Keep Standing!!! Live!!!

Love, LaQuanda B

Acknowledgements

I first want to give thanks and honor to God who is my life. Without him, I am nothing. I thank God for allowing me to make it through this journey disease free as it could have gone another way. Whoa....I thank my loving and wonderful grandparents Ezell and Dora Brown who helped my mother in raising me until I was thirteen years old. Their home was where it all started. May they continue to rest in peace. To the woman who birthed me, Jeanette "Netta" Brown-Farmer, into this world, I thank you for all of the sacrifices you made for me to ensure that I had the best in life. To my earthly father, Terry Leggett Jr, I thank you for showing me how a man is supposed to treat a woman and for taking care of me when you did. I will never forget! Thank you for giving me a brother whom I love dearly, Terry Leggett III and a wonderful 2nd mom who never showed any difference towards me...I love you

Francine Leggett. To every leader that I have sat under, you know who you are. I thank you for instilling in me Godly principles that have helped mold me into the woman I am today. To my ex-husband, Jason "Marco" George, Sr, if I had to do it all over again, I would, because you were a part of the plan in helping me get to the place I am now. So, I say thank you for playing your part so well. It taught me how to be a great wife, and without you, I wouldn't have had the three beautiful children we have now. I pray you well. To my ex-husband's family, I thank you all for continuing to accept me during a very dark place in my life. You all didn't have to remain in touch with me and your actions of caring will never go unnoticed. R.I.P to Tara& Helen! To each of my children, Jason, Jawan, and JaKiah George. I love each of you with all of my being. You were worth it all. I'm proud of each of you. WE SURVIVED. To my daughter, Montyshia Brabson, marrying your father is not the only reason that I'm here for you. I really do love you. To Tyanqua Carter-George, my daughter-in-love, thank you for giving me two beautiful grandchildren, Ai'Jah and Juan'ye. I'm forever blessed to be alive to witness these moments. To my beautiful best friends since kindergarten and middle school, Tracy Mays-Gibson & Mary Manning and Elayssandria Lacy, Tameka Stephen, Wilhelmina Lewis...I thank God for placing you ladies in my life and being the sisters that I never had. Our friendships are indeed true and is a true definition of the word "FRIEND"! You all rode this thang out with me from day 1, and though I knew you didn't like the situation that I was in, you didn't throw me away. Love is what love does. BFF's 4 EVA…. What Up Doe!!!! And last but not least, to the man who waited just for me. My wonderful, loving, handsome husband Jesse Ray Brabson, Jr. "Jay"/"JB", it was worth the wait. Thank you for loving God more than you love me. We were indeed the missing piece in each other's life. Thank you for loving my children, our children, like your own. Though we are far from perfect, **we are perfect for each other. And thank you for making me feel like my heart was never broken.**

    Love, LaQuanda E. Leggett- Brabson

Additional Reading

Below are selected Bible verses that help emphasize the story.

(Italic words are words spoken by Jesus)

(1). **Jeremiah 29:11** for I know the plans I have for you, "declares the Lord," plans to prosper you and not to harm you, plans to give you hope and a future **(NIV).**

(2). **Job 10:12** Thou has granted me life and favour, and thy visitation hath preserved my spirit. **(KJV)**

(3). **1st Corinthians 7:9** But if they cannot contain, let them marry: for it is better to marry than to burn. **(KJV)**

(4). **1st Corinthians 10:13** There hath no temptation taken you but such as is common to man: but God is faithful, who will not suffer you to be tempted above that ye are able; but will with the temptation also make a way to escape, that ye may be able to bear it. **(KJV)**

(5). **Matthew 5:27-29** *"You have heard that it was said, 'YOU SHALL NOT COMMIT ADULTERY';* **(28)** *but I say to you that everyone who* [so much as] *looks at a woman with lust for her has already committed adultery with her in his heart.* **(29)** *If your right eye makes you stumble and leads you to sin, tear it out and throw it away* [that is, remove yourself from the source of temptation]; *for it is better for you to lose one of the parts of your body, than for your whole body to be thrown into hell.* **(AMP)** words originally in red

(6). **Proverbs 3:5-6** Trust God from the bottom of your heart; don't try to figure out everything on your own. **(6)** Listen for God's voice in everything you do, everywhere you go; he's the one who will keep you on track. **(MSG)**

(7). **Psalms 119:133** Establish my footsteps in [the way of] Your word; Do not let any human weakness have power over me [causing me to be separated from You]. **(AMP)**

(8). **James 1:3-4** Be assured that the testing of your faith [through experience] produces endurance [leading to spiritual maturity, and inner peace]. **(4)** And let endurance have its perfect result and do a thorough work, so that you may be perfect and completely developed [in your faith], lacking in nothing. **(AMP)**

(9). **1st Corinthians 10:21-22** And you can't have it both ways, banqueting with the Master one day and slumming with demons the next. Besides, the master won't put up with it. He wants us-all or nothing. Do you think you can get off with anything less? **(MSG)**

(10). **Psalms 37:4-5** Delight thyself also in the Lord; and he shall give thee the desires of thine heart. **(5)** Commit thy way unto the Lord; trust also in him; and he shall bring it to pass. **(KJV) / Proverbs 10:22-23** The blessing of the Lord brings wealth, without painful toil for it. **(23)** A fool finds pleasure in wicked schemes, but a person of understanding delights in wisdom. **(NIV)**

(11). **Galatians 5:1** Christ has set us free to live a free life. So take your stand! Never again let anyone put a harness of slavery on you. *(MSG)*

(12). **Galatians 5:16-21** So I say, walk by the Spirit, and you will not gratify the desires of the flesh. **(17)** For the flesh desires what is contrary to the Spirit, and the Spirit what is contrary to the Flesh. they are in conflict with each other, so that you are not to do whatever you want. **(18)** But is you are led by the Spirit, you are not under the law. **(19)** The acts of the flesh are obvious: sexual immorality, impurity and debauchery; **(20)** idolatry and witchcraft; hatred, discord, jealousy, fits of rage, selfish ambition, dissensions, factions **(21)** and envy; drunkenness, orgies, and the like. I warn you, as I did before, that those who live like this will not inherit the kingdom of god. **(NIV)**/

Ephesians 6:11-12 put on the full armor of God, so that you can take your stand against the devil's schemes. **(12)** Four our struggle is not against flesh and blood, but against the authorities, against the powers of this dark world and against the spiritual forces of evil in the heavenly realms. **(NIV)**

(13). **James 1:5-8** If any of you lacks wisdom, you should ask God, who gives generously to all without finding fault, and it will be given to you. **(6)** But when you ask, you must believe and not doubt, because the one who doubts is like a wave of the sea, blown and tossed by the wind. **(7)** That person should not expect to receive anything from the Lord. **(8)** Such a person is double-minded and unstable in all they do. **(NIV)**

(14). **Philippians 4:6** Do not be anxious or worried about anything, but in everything [every circumstance and situation] by prayer and petition with thanksgiving, continue to make your [specific] requests known to God. **(AMP)**

(15). **James 3:10** Out of the same mouth come both blessing and cursing. these things, my brothers, should not be this way [for we have a moral obligation to speak in a manner that reflects our fear of God and profound respect for His people]. **(AMP)**

(16). **John 14:13** *And whatsoever ye shall ask in my name, that will I do, that the Father may be glorified in the Son.* **(KJV)** *words originally in red*

(17). **Proverbs 18:22** Whoso findeth a wife findeth a good thing, and obtaineth favour of the Lord. **(KJV)**

(18). **Hebrews 13:4** Marriage should be honored by all, and the marriage bed kept pure, for God will judge the adulterer and all the sexually immoral. **(NIV)**

(19). Song Insert

(19b). **Isaiah 55:8-9** For my thoughts are not your thoughts, neither are your ways my ways, saith the Lord. **(9)** For as the heavens are higher than the earth, so are my ways higher than your ways, and my thoughts than your thoughts. **(KJV)**

(20). **James 5:16** Confess your faults one to another, and pray one for another, that ye may be healed. The effectual fervent prayer of a righteous man availeth much. **(KJV)**

(21). **2nd Corinthians 9:7-8** Let each one give [thoughtfully and with purpose] just as he has decided in his heart, not grudgingly or under compulsion, for God loves a cheerful giver [and delights in the one whose heart is in his gift]. **(8)** And God is able to make all grace [every favor and earthly blessing] come in abundance to you, so that you may always [under all circumstances, regardless of the need] have complete sufficiency in everything [being completely self-sufficient in Him], and have an abundance for every good work and act of charity. **(AMP)**

(22). **Nehemiah 8:10** Nehemiah said,; Go and enjoy choice food and sweet drinks, and send some to those who have nothing prepared. This day is holy to our Lord. Do not grieve, for the joy of the Lord is your strength." **(NIV)**

(23). **Romans 12:2** And do not be conformed to this world [any longer with its superficial values and customs], but be transformed and progressively changed [as you mature spiritually] by the renewing of your mind [focusing on godly values and ethical attitudes], so that you may prove [for yourselves] what the will of God is, that which is good and acceptable and perfect [in His plan and purpose for you]. **(AMP)**

(24). **Philippians 4:7** And the peace of God, which passeth all understanding, shall keep your hearts and minds through Christ Jesus. **(KJV)**

(25). **Hebrews 11:1** Now faith is the substance of things hoped for, the evidence of things not seen. **(KJV)**

(26). **Proverbs 3:5-6** Trust in the Lord with all thine heart; and lean not unto thine own understanding. **(6)** In all thy ways acknowledge him, and he shall direct thy paths. **(KJV)**

(27). **Romans 8:18** For I consider [from the standpoint of faith] that the sufferings of the present life are not worthy to be compared with the glory that is about to be revealed to us and in us! **(AMP)**

(28). **Hebrews 12:1-3** Therefore, since we are surrounded by so great a cloud of witnesses [who by faith have testified to the truth of God's absolute faithfulness], stripping off every unnecessary weight and sin which so easily and cleverly entangles us, let us run with endurance and active persistence the race that is set before us, **(2)** [looking away from all that will distract us and] focusing our eyes on Jesus, who is the Author and Perfecter of faith [the first incentive for our belief to maturity], who for the joy [of accomplishing the goal] set before Him endured the cross, disregarding the shame, and sat down at the right hand of the throne of God [revealing His deity, His authority, and the completion of His work]. **(3)** Just consider and meditate on Him who endured from sinners such bitter hostility against Himself [consider it all in comparison with your trials], so that you will not grow weary and lose heart. **(AMP)/ Acts 9:15-16** But the Lord said unto him, *Go thy way: for he is a chosen vessel unto me, to bear my name before the Gentiles, and kings, and the children of Israel: (16) For I will shew him how great* *things he must suffer for my name's sake.* **(KJV)** *words originally in red*

About the Author

LaQuanda E Leggett Brabson was born and raised in Detroit, Michigan. She survived an abusive marriage of emotional, mental, physical, and verbal abuse. She is the proud mother of four children 26, 21, 20. and 16; three that she birthed and one from marriage. She also has two beautiful grandchildren who she spoils without guilt! She now resides in Knoxville, Tennessee, where she is married to a wonderful man of God who serves alongside her as a licensed minister of the Gospel. She is a licensed cosmetologist and owner of Royal Favor Hair Salon as well as a Certified Clinical Medical Assistant studying to become a nurse. She is the Co-Founder of the non-profit organization, Beauty for Ashes 4 Life with her best friend, which serves women battling cancer or cancer survivors as well as domestic violence and abuse victims.

Contact Information:

brokengracefully1.com

@brokengracefully on Facebook

beautyforashes4life.com

Beauty For Ashes 4 Life on Facebook

Detroit Area (313) 312-2193

Knoxville Area (734) 288-8682

All are welcome to contact either numbers for help

All Donations Are Welcomed

Made in the USA
Coppell, TX
31 December 2019